Detecting
Women
Pocket Guide
3rd edition

Also by **Willetta L. Heising**

Detecting Women, 3rd edition
Detecting Men
Detecting Men Pocket Guide
Detecting Women 2
Detecting Women 2 Pocket Guide
Detecting Women

Detecting Women Pocket Guide

3rd edition

Checklist for Mystery Series Written by Women

Willetta L. Heising

PURPLE
MOON
PRESS

Detecting Women
Pocket Guide
3rd edition
Checklist for Mystery Series
Written by Women

Willetta L. Heising

 Purple Moon Press
PURPLE 3319 Greenfield Rd., Suite 317
MOON
PRESS Dearborn, Michigan 48120-1212

voice: 313-593-1033
fax: 313-593-4087
e-mail: purplemoon@prodigy.net

Distribution
Purple Moon Press books are distributed to the book
trade by Partners Books, 2325 Jarco Drive, PO Box 580,
Holt, Michigan 48842. Call toll-free 1-800-336-3137. Also
available from Ingram Book Company and Baker & Taylor.
Resellers outside the book trade should contact Purple
Moon Press.

Notice of Rights

ISBN: 0-9644593-7-X

Cover illustration by Bill Holbrook.
Cover design by Chris Shamus.
Electronic prepress, text and interior design by
Jacqué Consulting & Design of Dearborn, Michigan.
Printed and bound in the USA by Malloy Lithographing
of Ann Arbor, Michigan.

First printing October 1998

'Tis the good reader
that makes the good book.

Ralph Waldo Emerson
"Success," *Conduct of Life* (1860)

Pocket Guidelines

This Pocket Guide Checklist for Mystery Series Written by Women is designed as a companion to the full-size edition of *Detecting Women*. Owing to its small size, the pocket guide includes "just the facts"—author name (last name first), name of the continuing character, numbered book titles in correct series order, publication date, major mystery awards and nominations, and alternative titles.

For the most part, *Detecting Women* presents only living authors who write series characters. However, two authors who died in 1998 have been included. More than 1100 titles in 102 series from 69 women authors who are no longer living can be found in *Detecting Women 2* and the Detecting *Women 2 Pocket Guide*.

We have adopted a two-book minimum requirement for listing in the 3rd edition of *Detecting Women*, owing to the large number of new women mystery authors since our last edition in 1996. However, if an established series author has a new series with only one novel, we have listed that new series as part of her complete entry.

Every series listing includes two blank unnumbered lines for future additions. In some cases, additions to the series will not be forthcoming, but you can use those lines for whatever appeals to you.

Author entries not previously appearing in *Detecting Women 2* are designated with a ❋ . Some new authors were inadvertently overlooked in the earlier edition, however, more than 60% of new authors listed here began publishing in 1996 or later.

Nonseries novels are not included in the Detecting Women data base. For this reason you will not find the psychological suspense novels of Ruth Rendell writing as Barbara Vine because these books do not feature continuing characters. Neither will you find such authors as Mary Higgins Clark or Minette Walters who write standalone novels.

Whenever a pseudonymous author is listed, you will find a [P] appearing after that name. The author's true identity is provided in the Chapter 7 of the full-size edition, along with a list of other pseudonyms she has used.

Dates of publication are the earliest dates of publication in English. These are not necessarily the U.S. dates of publication. Sometimes U.S. publication is delayed as many as three or four years after a book's first appearance in the U.K., Canada or Australia. And some books are never published in the United States. While U.S. editions typically appear in the year following their arrival in the U.K. or Canada, the works of some popular authors are published simultaneously around the world.

Starred titles identify mystery award winners and nominees. Solid stars ★ denote award winners and open stars ☆ indicate nominees. Complete awards information, including award type and category, is available in Chapter 8 of the full-text edition.

Two columns of check boxes are provided to record books you own and books you've read, or to keep score and rate your favorites. Some pocket guide users report sharing the pocket guide with a spouse or friend and keeping score to see who's read more titles.

Short story collections are listed whenever they feature a series character who also appears in full-length novels. If a character has thus far appeared only in short fiction collections, those anthologies are not listed, unless the author has other series of full-length novels.

If you have information regarding errors or omissions in *Detecting Women Pocket Guide* or the full-size edition, please send documentation to Purple Moon Press so that we can make the appropriate corrections.

Happy mystery reading!

ADAMS, Deborah
Jesus Creek TN
- ❑ ❑ 1 - All the Great Pretenders (1992)☆
- ❑ ❑ 2 - All the Crazy Winters (1992)
- ❑ ❑ 3 - All the Dark Disguises (1993)
- ❑ ❑ 4 - All the Hungry Mothers (1993)
- ❑ ❑ 5 - All the Deadly Beloved (1995)
- ❑ ❑ 6 - All the Blood Relations (1997)
- ❑ ❑ . . . .
- ❑ ❑ . . . .

ADAMS, Jane
Mike Croft
- ❑ ❑ 1 - The Greenway (1995)☆
- ❑ ❑ 2 - Cast the First Stone (1996)
- ❑ ❑ 3 - Fade to Grey (1998)
- ❑ ❑ . . . .
- ❑ ❑ . . . .

ADAMSON, M. J.
Balthazar Marten & Sixto Cardenas
- ❑ ❑ 1 - Not Till a Hot January (1987)
- ❑ ❑ 2 - A February Face (1987)
- ❑ ❑ 3 - Remember March (1988)
- ❑ ❑ 4 - April When They Woo (1988)
- ❑ ❑ 5 - May's Newfangled Mirth (1989)
- ❑ ❑ . . . .
- ❑ ❑ . . . .

AIRD, Catherine [P]
Christopher Dennis "Seedy" Sloan
- ❑ ❑ 1 - The Religious Body (1966)
- ❑ ❑ 2 - Henrietta Who? (1968)
- ❑ ❑ 3 - The Complete Steel (1969)
- ❑ ❑ - U.S.-The Stately Home Murder
- ❑ ❑ 4 - A Late Phoenix (1970)
- ❑ ❑ 5 - His Burial Too (1973)
- ❑ ❑ 6 - Slight Mourning (1975)
- ❑ ❑ 7 - Parting Breath (1977)
- ❑ ❑ 8 - Some Die Eloquent (1979)

❏ ❏   9 - Passing Strange (1980)
❏ ❏ 10 - Last Respects (1982)
❏ ❏ 11 - Harm's Way (1984)
❏ ❏ 12 - A Dead Liberty (1986)
❏ ❏ 13 - The Body Politic (1990)
❏ ❏ 14 - A Going Concern (1993)
❏ ❏ 15 - After Effects (1996)
❏ ❏   ss - Injury Time [16 stories] (1997)
❏ ❏ 16 - Stiff News (1998)
❏ ❏ . . . .
❏ ❏ . . . .

ALBERT, Susan Wittig

China Bayles

❏ ❏ 1 - Thyme of Death (1992)☆☆
❏ ❏ 2 - Witches' Bane (1993)
❏ ❏ 3 - Hangman's Root (1994)
❏ ❏ 4 - Rosemary Remembered (1995)
❏ ❏ 5 - Rueful Death (1996)
❏ ❏ 6 - Love Lies Bleeding (1997)
❏ ❏ 7 - Chile Death (1998)
❏ ❏ . . . .
❏ ❏ . . . .

ALEXANDER, Skye

Charlotte McCrae

❏ ❏ 1 - Hidden Agenda (1997)★
❏ ❏ 2 - Hide in Plain Sight (1999)
❏ ❏ 3 - Rose-Colored Glasses (2000)
❏ ❏ . . . .
❏ ❏ . . . .

ALLEN, Irene [P]

Elizabeth Elliot

❏ ❏ 1 - Quaker Silence (1992)
❏ ❏ 2 - Quaker Witness (1993)
❏ ❏ 3 - Quaker Testimony (1996)
❏ ❏ 4 - Quaker Indictment (1998)
❏ ❏ . . . .
❏ ❏ . . . .

ALLEN, Kate [P]
Alison Kaine
- ❏ ❏ 1 - Tell Me What You Like (1993)
- ❏ ❏ 2 - Give My Secrets Back (1995)
- ❏ ❏ 3 - Takes One to Know One (1996)
- ❏ ❏ 4 - Just a Little Lie (1998)
- ❏ ❏ . . . .
- ❏ ❏ . . . .

AMATO, Angela
and Joe Sharkey
Gerry Conte
- ❏ ❏ 1 - LadyGold (1998)
- ❏ ❏ 2 - Jackpot (1999)
- ❏ ❏ . . . .
- ❏ ❏ . . . .

AMEY, Linda
Blair Emerson
- ❏ ❏ 1 - Bury Her Sweetly (1992)
- ❏ ❏ 2 - At Dead of Night (1995)
- ❏ ❏ . . . .
- ❏ ❏ . . . .

ANDREAE, Christine
Lee Squires
- ❏ ❏ 1 - Trail of Murder (1992)☆
- ❏ ❏ 2 - Grizzly, A Murder (1994)
- ❏ ❏ 3 - A Small Target (1996)
- ❏ ❏ . . . .
- ❏ ❏ . . . .

ANDREWS, Sarah
Em Hansen
- ❏ ❏ 1 - Tensleep (1994)
- ❏ ❏ 2 - A Fall in Denver (1995)
- ❏ ❏ 3 - Mother Nature (1997)
- ❏ ❏ 4 - Only Flesh and Bones (1998)
- ❏ ❏ . . . .
- ❏ ❏ . . . .

ARNOLD, Catherine [P]
Karen Perry-Mondori
- ❏ ❏ 1 - Due Process (1996)
- ❏ ❏ 2 - Imperfect Justice (1997)
- ❏ ❏ 3 - Wrongful Death (1998)
- ❏ ❏ . . . .
- ❏ ❏ . . . .

ARNOLD, Margot [P]
Penny Spring & Toby Glendower
- ❏ ❏ 1 - Exit Actors, Dying (1979)
- ❏ ❏ 2 - Zadock's Treasure (1979)
- ❏ ❏ 3 - The Cape Cod Caper (1980)
- ❏ ❏ 4 - Death of a Voodoo Doll (1982)
- ❏ ❏ 5 - Lament for a Lady Laird (1982)
- ❏ ❏ 6 - Death on a Dragon's Tongue (1982)
- ❏ ❏ 7 - The Menehune Murders (1989)
- ❏ ❏ 8 - Toby's Folly (1990)
- ❏ ❏ 9 - The Catacomb Conspiracy (1991)
- ❏ ❏ 10 - Cape Cod Conundrum (1992)
- ❏ ❏ 11 - Dirge for a Dorset Druid (1994)
- ❏ ❏ 12 - The Midas Murders (1995)
- ❏ ❏ . . . .
- ❏ ❏ . . . .

ATHERTON, Nancy
Aunt Dimity
- ❏ ❏ 1 - Aunt Dimity's Death (1992)
- ❏ ❏ 2 - Aunt Dimity and the Duke (1994)
- ❏ ❏ 3 - Aunt Dimity's Good Deed (1996)
- ❏ ❏ 4 - Aunt Dimity Digs In (1998)
- ❏ ❏ . . . .
- ❏ ❏ . . . .

AYRES, Noreen
Samantha "Smokey" Brandon
- ❏ ❏ 1 - A World the Color of Salt (1992)
- ❏ ❏ 2 - Carcass Trade (1994)
- ❏ ❏ . . . .
- ❏ ❏ . . . .

BABBIN, Jacqueline

Clovis Kelly

❑ ❑ 1 - Prime Time Corpse (1972)
❑ ❑   - APA-Bloody Special (1989)
❑ ❑ 2 - Bloody Soaps (1989)
❑ ❑ . . . .
❑ ❑ . . . .

BABSON, Marian

Douglas Perkins

❑ ❑ 1 - Cover-up Story (1971)
❑ ❑ 2 - Murder on Show (1972)
❑ ❑   - U.S.-Murder at the Cat Show (1989)
❑ ❑ 3 - Tourists are for Trapping (1989)
❑ ❑ 4 - In the Teeth of Adversity (1990)
❑ ❑ . . . .
❑ ❑ . . . .

Eve Sinclair & Trixie Dolan

❑ ❑ 1 - Reel Murder (1986)
❑ ❑ 2 - Encore Murder (1989)
❑ ❑ 3 - Shadows in Their Blood (1993)
❑ ❑ 4 - Even Yuppies Die (1993)
❑ ❑ 5 - Break a Leg Darlings (1995)
❑ ❑ . . . .
❑ ❑ . . . .

BACON-SMITH, Camille

Kevin Bradley

❑ ❑ 1 - Eye of the Daemon (1996)
❑ ❑ 2 - Eyes of the Empress (1998)
❑ ❑ . . . .
❑ ❑ . . . .

BAILEY, Michele

Mathilda Haycastle

❑ ❑ 1 - Dreadful Lies (1994)
❑ ❑ 2 - The Cuckoo Case (1995)
❑ ❑ 3 - Haycastle's Cricket (1996)
❑ ❑ . . . .
❑ ❑ . . . .

BAKER, Nikki [P]
Virginia Kelly
❏ ❏　1 - In the Game (1991)
❏ ❏　2 - The Lavender House Murder (1992)
❏ ❏　3 - Long Goodbyes (1993)
❏ ❏　. . . . .
❏ ❏　. . . . .

BANKS, Carolyn
Robin Vaughan
❏ ❏　1 - Death by Dressage (1993)
❏ ❏　2 - Groomed for Death (1994)
❏ ❏　3 - Murder Well-Bred (1995)
❏ ❏　4 - Death on the Diagonal (1996)
❏ ❏　5 - A Horse To Die For (1996)
❏ ❏　. . . . .
❏ ❏　. . . . .

BANKS, Jackie
Ruby Gordon
❏ ❏　1 - Maid in the Shade (1998)
❏ ❏　2 - Barely Maid (1999)
❏ ❏　. . . . .
❏ ❏　. . . . .

BANNISTER, Jo
Clio Rees & Harry Marsh
❏ ❏　1 - Striving With Gods (1984)
❏ ❏　2 - Gilgamesh (1989)
❏ ❏　3 - The Going Down of the Sun (1990)
❏ ❏　. . . . .
❏ ❏　. . . . .

Frank Shapiro, Cal Donovan & Liz Graham
❏ ❏　1 - A Bleeding of Innocents (1993)
❏ ❏　2 - Sins of the Heart (1994)
❏ ❏　　- U.S.-Charisma
❏ ❏　3 - Burning Desires (1995)
❏ ❏　　- U.S.-A Taste for Burning
❏ ❏　4 - No Birds Sing (1996)

❑ ❑   5 - Broken Lines (1998)
❑ ❑   6 - The Hireling's Tale (1999)
❑ ❑   . . . .
❑ ❑   . . . .

Mickey Flynn

❑ ❑   1 - Shards (1990)
❑ ❑   2 - Death and Other Lovers (1991)
❑ ❑   . . . .
❑ ❑   . . . .

Primrose Holland

❑ ❑   1 - The Primrose Convention (1998)
❑ ❑   . . . .
❑ ❑   . . . .

BARNES, Linda

Carlotta Carlyle

❑ ❑   1 - A Trouble of Fools (1987)★☆☆☆
❑ ❑   2 - The Snake Tattoo (1989)
❑ ❑   3 - Coyote (1990)
❑ ❑   4 - Steel Guitar (1991)
❑ ❑   5 - Snapshot (1993)
❑ ❑   6 - Hardware (1995)
❑ ❑   7 - Cold Case (1997)
❑ ❑   . . . .
❑ ❑   . . . .

Michael Spraggue

❑ ❑   1 - Blood Will Have Blood (1982)
❑ ❑   2 - Bitter Finish (1983)
❑ ❑   3 - Dead Heat (1984)
❑ ❑   4 - Cities of the Dead (1986)
❑ ❑   . . . .
❑ ❑   . . . .

BARR, Nevada

Anna Pigeon

❑ ❑   1 - Track of the Cat (1993)★★
❑ ❑   2 - A Superior Death (1994)
❑ ❑   3 - Ill Wind (1995)

❏ ❏   4 - Firestorm (1996)
❏ ❏   5 - Endangered Species (1997)
❏ ❏   6 - Blind Descent (1998)
❏ ❏   7 - Liberty Falling (1999)
❏ ❏   . . . .
❏ ❏   . . . .

BARRETT, Kathleen Anne

Beth Hartley

❏ ❏   1 - Milwaukee Winters Can Be Murder (1996)
❏ ❏   2 - Milwaukee Summers Can Be Deadly (1997)
❏ ❏   3 - Milwaukee Autumns Can Be Lethal (1998)
❏ ❏   . . . .
❏ ❏   . . . .

BARRETT, Margaret [P] and Charles Dennis

Susan Given

❏ ❏   1 - Given the Crime (1998)
❏ ❏   2 - Given the Evidence (1998)
❏ ❏   . . . .
❏ ❏   . . . .

BARRON, Stephanie [P]

Jane Austen

❏ ❏   1 - Jane and the Unpleasantness at Scargrave Manor (1996)
❏ ❏   2 - Jane and the Man of the Cloth (1997)
❏ ❏   3 - Jane and the Wandering Eye (1998)
❏ ❏   . . . .
❏ ❏   . . . .

BARTHOLOMEW, Nancy

Sierra Lavotini

❏ ❏   1 - The Miracle Strip (1998)
❏ ❏   2 - Dragstrip (1999)
❏ ❏   . . . .
❏ ❏   . . . .

BEATON, M. C. [P]

Agatha Raisin

- ❏ ❏ 1 - Agatha Raisin and the Quiche of Death (1992)
- ❏ ❏ 2 - Agatha Raisin and the Vicious Vet (1993)
- ❏ ❏ 3 - ...and the Potted Gardener (1994)
- ❏ ❏ 4 - ...and the Walkers of Dembley (1995)
- ❏ ❏ 5 - ...and the Murderous Marriage (1996)
- ❏ ❏ 6 - ...and the Terrible Tourist (1997)
- ❏ ❏ 7 - ...and the Wellspring of Death (1998)
- ❏ ❏ 8 - ...and the Wizard of Evesham (1999)
- ❏ ❏ . . . .
- ❏ ❏ . . . .

Hamish Macbeth

- ❏ ❏ 1 - Death of a Gossip (1985)
- ❏ ❏ 2 - Death of a Cad (1987)
- ❏ ❏ 3 - Death of an Outsider (1988)
- ❏ ❏ 4 - Death of a Perfect Wife (1989)
- ❏ ❏ 5 - Death of a Hussy (1990)
- ❏ ❏ 6 - Death of a Snob (1991)
- ❏ ❏ 7 - Death of a Prankster (1992)
- ❏ ❏ 8 - Death of a Glutton (1993)
- ❏ ❏ 9 - Death of a Travelling Man (1993)
- ❏ ❏ 10 - Death of a Charming Man (1994)
- ❏ ❏ 11 - Death of a Nag (1995)
- ❏ ❏ 12 - Death of a Macho Man (1996)
- ❏ ❏ 13 - Death of a Dentist (1997)
- ❏ ❏ 14 - Death of a Scriptwriter (1998)
- ❏ ❏ . . . .
- ❏ ❏ . . . .

BEAUFORT, Simon [P]

new

Geoffrey de Mappestone

- ❏ ❏ 1 - Murder in the Holy City (1998)
- ❏ ❏ 2 - A Head for Poisoning (1999)
- ❏ ❏ . . . .
- ❏ ❏ . . . .

BECK, K. K.

Iris Cooper

❏ ❏   1 - Death in a Deck Chair (1984)
❏ ❏   2 - Murder in a Mummy Case (1985)
❏ ❏   3 - Peril Under the Palms (1989)
❏ ❏   . . . .
❏ ❏   . . . .

Jane da Silva

❏ ❏   1 - A Hopeless Case (1992)
❏ ❏   2 - Amateur Night (1993)
❏ ❏   3 - Electric City (1994)
❏ ❏   4 - Cold Smoked (1995)
❏ ❏   . . . .
❏ ❏   . . . .

BEDFORD, Jean

Anna Southwood

❏ ❏   1 - To Make a Killing (1990)
❏ ❏   2 - Worse Than Death (1992)
❏ ❏   3 - Signs of Murder (1993)
❏ ❏   . . . .
❏ ❏   . . . .

BEECHAM, Rose

Amanda Valentine

❏ ❏   1 - Introducing Amanda Valentine (1992)
❏ ❏   2 - Second Guess (1994)
❏ ❏   3 - Fair Play (1995)
❏ ❏   . . . .
❏ ❏   . . . .

BELFORT, Sophie [P]

Molly Rafferty

❏ ❏   1 - The Lace Curtain Murders (1986)
❏ ❏   2 - The Marvell College Murders (1991)
❏ ❏   3 - Eyewitness to Murder (1992)
❏ ❏   . . . .
❏ ❏   . . . .

BELL, Nancy
Biggie Weatherford & J. R.
- ❏ ❏ 1 - Biggie and the Poisoned Politician (1996)☆
- ❏ ❏ 2 - Biggie and the Mangled Mortician (1997)
- ❏ ❏ 3 - Biggie and the Fricasseed Fat Man (1998)
- ❏ ❏ . . . .
- ❏ ❏ . . . .

BELL, Pauline
Benny Mitchell
- ❏ ❏ 1 - The Dead Do Not Praise (1990)
- ❏ ❏ 2 - Feast into Mourning (1991)
- ❏ ❏ 3 - No Pleasure in Death (1992)
- ❏ ❏ 4 - The Way of a Serpent (1993)
- ❏ ❏ 5 - Downhill to Death (1994)
- ❏ ❏ 6 - Sleeping Partners (1995)
- ❏ ❏ 7 - A Multitude of Sins (1997)
- ❏ ❏ 8 - Blood Ties (1998)
- ❏ ❏ . . . .
- ❏ ❏ . . . .

BENJAMIN, Carole Lea
Rachel Alexander & Dash
- ❏ ❏ 1 - This Dog for Hire (1996)☆
- ❏ ❏ 2 - The Dog Who Knew Too Much (1997)
- ❏ ❏ 3 - A Hell of a Dog (1998)
- ❏ ❏ . . . .
- ❏ ❏ . . . .

BENKE, Patricia D.
Judith Thornton
- ❏ ❏ 1 - Guilty By Choice (1995)
- ❏ ❏ 2 - False Witness (1996)
- ❏ ❏ 3 - Above the Law (1997)
- ❏ ❏ . . . .
- ❏ ❏ . . . .

BENNETT, Liza

Peg Goodenough

❑ ❑   1 - Madison Avenue Murder (1989)
❑ ❑   2 - Seventh Avenue Murder (1990)
❑ ❑   . . . .
❑ ❑   . . . .

BERENSON, Laurien

Melanie Travis

❑ ❑   1 - A Pedigree to Die For (1995)
❑ ❑   2 - Underdog (1996)
❑ ❑   3 - Dog Eat Dog (1996)
❑ ❑   4 - Hair of the Dog (1997)
❑ ❑   5 - Watchdog (1998)
❑ ❑   6 - Hush Puppy (1999)
❑ ❑   . . . .
❑ ❑   . . . .

BERNE, Karin [P]

Ellie Gordon

❑ ❑   1 - Bare Acquaintances (1985)
❑ ❑   2 - Shock Value (1985)
❑ ❑   3 - False Impressions (1986)
❑ ❑   . . . .
❑ ❑   . . . .

BERRY, Carole

Bonnie Indermill

❑ ❑   1 - The Letter of the Law (1987)
❑ ❑   2 - The Year of the Monkey (1988)
❑ ❑   3 - Good Night, Sweet Prince (1990)
❑ ❑   4 - Island Girl (1991)
❑ ❑   5 - The Death of a Difficult Woman (1994)
❑ ❑   6 - The Death of a Dancing Fool (1996)
❑ ❑   7 - Death of a Dimpled Darling (1997)
❑ ❑   . . . .
❑ ❑   . . . .

BISHOP, Claudia [P]
Sarah & Meg Quilliam
- ❏ ❏   1 - A Taste for Murder (1994)
- ❏ ❏   2 - A Dash of Death (1995)
- ❏ ❏   3 - A Pinch of Poison (1995)
- ❏ ❏   4 - Murder Well-Done (1996)
- ❏ ❏   5 - Death Dines Out (1997)
- ❏ ❏   6 - A Touch of the Grape (1998)
- ❏ ❏   . . . .
- ❏ ❏   . . . .

BLACK, Cara
Aimee Leduc
- ❏ ❏   1 - Murder in the Marais (1999)
- ❏ ❏   2 - Murder in the Chabris (2000)
- ❏ ❏   . . . .
- ❏ ❏   . . . .

BLACK, Veronica [P]
Joan, Sister
- ❏ ❏   1 - A Vow of Silence (1990)
- ❏ ❏   2 - A Vow of Chastity (1992)
- ❏ ❏   3 - A Vow of Sanctity (1993)
- ❏ ❏   4 - A Vow of Obedience (1993)
- ❏ ❏   5 - A Vow of Penance (1994)
- ❏ ❏   6 - A Vow of Devotion (1994)
- ❏ ❏   7 - A Vow of Fidelity (1995)
- ❏ ❏   8 - A Vow of Poverty (1996)
- ❏ ❏   9 - A Vow of Adoration (1997)
- ❏ ❏ 10 - A Vow of Compassion (1998)
- ❏ ❏   . . . .
- ❏ ❏   . . . .

BLANC, Suzanne
Miguel Menendez
- ❏ ❏   1 - The Green Stone (1961)★
- ❏ ❏   2 - The Yellow Villa (1964)
- ❏ ❏   3 - The Rose Window (1967)
- ❏ ❏   . . . .
- ❏ ❏   . . . .

BLAND, Eleanor Taylor

Marti MacAlister

- ❏ ❏ 1 - Dead Time (1992)
- ❏ ❏ 2 - Slow Burn (1993)
- ❏ ❏ 3 - Gone Quiet (1994)
- ❏ ❏ 4 - Done Wrong (1995)
- ❏ ❏ 5 - Keep Still (1996)
- ❏ ❏ 6 - See No Evil (1998)
- ❏ ❏ 7 - Tell No Tales (1999)
- ❏ ❏ ....
- ❏ ❏ ....

BLOCK, Barbara

Robin Light

- ❏ ❏ 1 - Chutes and Adders (1994)
- ❏ ❏ 2 - Twister (1994)
- ❏ ❏ 3 - In Plain Sight (1996)
- ❏ ❏ 4 - The Scent of Murder (1997)
- ❏ ❏ 5 - Vanishing Act (1998)
- ❏ ❏ ....
- ❏ ❏ ....

BOLITHO, Janie

Ian Roper

- ❏ ❏ 1 - Kindness Can Kill (1993)
- ❏ ❏ 2 - Ripe for Revenge (1994)
- ❏ ❏ 3 - Motive for Murder (1994)
- ❏ ❏ 4 - Dangerous Deceit (1995)
- ❏ ❏ 5 - Finger of Fate (1996)
- ❏ ❏ 6 - Sequence of Shame (1996)
- ❏ ❏ 7 - Absence of Angels (1997)
- ❏ ❏ 8 - Exposure of Evil (1998)
- ❏ ❏ ....
- ❏ ❏ ....

Rose Trevelyan

- ❏ ❏ 1 - Snapped in Cornwall (1997)
- ❏ ❏ 2 - Framed in Cornwall (1998)
- ❏ ❏ ....
- ❏ ❏ ....

BORTHWICK, J. S. [P]
Sarah Deane & Alex McKenzie
- ❏ ❏ 1 - The Case of the Hook-Billed Kites (1982)
- ❏ ❏ 2 - The Down East Murders (1985)
- ❏ ❏ 3 - The Student Body (1986)
- ❏ ❏ 4 - Bodies of Water (1990)
- ❏ ❏ 5 - Dude on Arrival (1992)
- ❏ ❏ 6 - The Bridled Groom (1994)
- ❏ ❏ 7 - Dolly Is Dead (1995)
- ❏ ❏ 8 - The Garden Plot (1997)
- ❏ ❏ 9 - My Body Lies Over the Ocean (1999)
- ❏ ❏ . . . .
- ❏ ❏ . . . .

BORTON, D. B. [P]
Cat Caliban
- ❏ ❏ 1 - One for the Money (1993)
- ❏ ❏ 2 - Two Points for Murder (1993)
- ❏ ❏ 3 - Three Is a Crowd (1994)
- ❏ ❏ 4 - Four Elements of Murder (1995)
- ❏ ❏ 5 - Five Alarm Fire (1996)
- ❏ ❏ 6 - Six Feet Under (1997)
- ❏ ❏ . . . .
- ❏ ❏ . . . .

Gilda Liberty
- ❏ ❏ 1 - Fade to Black [as Della Borton] (1999)
- ❏ ❏ . . . .
- ❏ ❏ . . . .

BOWEN, Gail
Joanne Kilbourn
- ❏ ❏ 1 - Deadly Appearances (1990)
- ❏ ❏ 2 - Love and Murder (1991)
- ❏ ❏ - APA-Murder at the Mendel
- ❏ ❏ 3 - The Wandering Soul Murders (1993)
- ❏ ❏ 4 - A Colder Kind of Death (1994)★
- ❏ ❏ 5 - A Killing Spring (1996)
- ❏ ❏ 6 - A Verdict in Blood (1998)
- ❏ ❏ . . . .
- ❏ ❏ . . . .

BOWEN, Rhys [P]
Evan Evans
- ❏ ❏   1 - Evans Above (1997)
- ❏ ❏   2 - Evan Help Us (1998)
- ❏ ❏   3 - Evanly Choirs (1999)
- ❏ ❏   . . . .
- ❏ ❏   . . . .

BOWERS, Elisabeth
Meg Lacey
- ❏ ❏   1 - Ladies' Night (1988)
- ❏ ❏   2 - No Forwarding Address (1991)
- ❏ ❏   . . . .
- ❏ ❏   . . . .

BOYLAN, Eleanor
Clara Gamadge
- ❏ ❏   1 - Working Murder (1989)☆
- ❏ ❏   2 - Murder Observed (1990)
- ❏ ❏   3 - Murder Machree (1992)
- ❏ ❏   4 - Pushing Murder (1993)
- ❏ ❏   5 - Murder Crossed (1996)
- ❏ ❏   . . . .
- ❏ ❏   . . . .

BRAUN, Lilian Jackson
Jim Qwilleran, Koko & Yum Yum
- ❏ ❏   1 - The Cat Who Could Read Backwards (1966)
- ❏ ❏   2 - The Cat Who Ate Danish Modern (1967)
- ❏ ❏   3 - The Cat Who Turned On and Off (1968)
- ❏ ❏   4 - The Cat Who Saw Red (1986)☆
- ❏ ❏   5 - The Cat Who Played Brahms (1987)☆
- ❏ ❏   6 - The Cat Who Played Post Office (1987)
- ❏ ❏   7 - The Cat Who Knew Shakespeare (1988)
- ❏ ❏   8 - The Cat Who Sniffed Glue (1988)
- ❏ ❏   9 - The Cat Who Went Underground (1989)
- ❏ ❏ 10 - The Cat Who Talked to Ghosts (1990)
- ❏ ❏ 11 - The Cat Who Lived High (1990)
- ❏ ❏ 12 - The Cat Who Knew a Cardinal (1991)
- ❏ ❏ 13 - The Cat Who Moved a Mountain (1992)

❏ ❏ 14 - The Cat Who Wasn't There (1993)
❏ ❏ 15 - The Cat Who Came to Breakfast (1994)
❏ ❏ 16 - The Cat Who Went into the Closet (1994)
❏ ❏ 17 - The Cat Who Blew the Whistle (1995)
❏ ❏ 18 - The Cat Who Said Cheese (1996)
❏ ❏ 19 - The Cat Who Tailed a Thief (1997)
❏ ❏ 20 - The Cat Who Sang for the Birds (1998)
❏ ❏ 21 - The Cat Who Saw Stars (1999)
❏ ❏ . . . .
❏ ❏ . . . .

BRENNAN, Carol

Emily Silver
❏ ❏ 1 - In the Dark (1994)
❏ ❏ 2 - Chill of Summer (1995)
❏ ❏ . . . .
❏ ❏ . . . .

Liz Wareham
❏ ❏ 1 - Headhunt (1991)
❏ ❏ 2 - Full Commission (1992)
❏ ❏ . . . .
❏ ❏ . . . .

BRIGHTWELL, Emily [P]

Insp. Witherspoon & Mrs. Jeffries
❏ ❏ 1 - The Inspector and Mrs. Jeffries (1993)
❏ ❏ 2 - Mrs. Jeffries Dusts for Clues (1993)
❏ ❏ 3 - The Ghost and Mrs. Jeffries (1993)
❏ ❏ 4 - Mrs. Jeffries Takes Stock (1994)
❏ ❏ 5 - Mrs. Jeffries on the Ball (1994)
❏ ❏ 6 - Mrs. Jeffries on the Trail (1995)
❏ ❏ 7 - Mrs. Jeffries Plays the Cook (1995)
❏ ❏ 8 - Mrs. Jeffries and the Missing Alibi (1996)
❏ ❏ 9 - Mrs. Jeffries Stands Corrected (1996)
❏ ❏ 10 - Mrs. Jeffries Takes the Stage (1997)
❏ ❏ 11 - Mrs. Jeffries Questions the Answer (1997)
❏ ❏ 12 - Mrs. Jeffries Reveals Her Art (1998)
❏ ❏ 13 - Mrs. Jeffries Takes the Cake (1998)
❏ ❏ . . . .
❏ ❏ . . . .

BRILL, Toni [P]
Midge Cohen
- ❏ ❏   1 - Date With a Dead Doctor (1991)
- ❏ ❏   2 - Date With a Plummeting Publisher (1993)
- ❏ ❏   . . . .
- ❏ ❏   . . . .

BROD, D. C.
Quint McCauley
- ❏ ❏   1 - Murder in Store (1989)
- ❏ ❏   2 - Error In Judgment (1990)
- ❏ ❏   3 - Masquerade in Blue (1991)
- ❏ ❏   - APA-Framed in Blue
- ❏ ❏   4 - Brothers in Blood (1993)
- ❏ ❏   . . . .
- ❏ ❏   . . . .

BROWN, Lizbie [P]
Elizabeth Blair
- ❏ ❏   1 - Broken Star (1992)
- ❏ ❏   2 - Turkey Tracks (1994)
- ❏ ❏   . . . .
- ❏ ❏   . . . .

BROWN, Molly
Aphra Behn
- ❏ ❏   1 - Invitation to a Funeral (1997)
- ❏ ❏   2 - The Lemon Juice Plot (2000)
- ❏ ❏   . . . .
- ❏ ❏   . . . .

BROWN, Rita Mae
Mary Minor Haristeen
- ❏ ❏   1 - Wish You Were Here (1990)
- ❏ ❏   2 - Rest in Pieces (1992)
- ❏ ❏   3 - Murder at Monticello (1994)
- ❏ ❏   4 - Pay Dirt (1995)

❏ ❏ 5 - Murder, She Meowed (1996)
❏ ❏ 6 - Murder on the Prowl (1998)
❏ ❏ . . . .
❏ ❏ . . . .

BRYAN, Kate [P]

Maggie Maguire

❏ ❏ 1 - Murder at Bent Elbow (1998)
❏ ❏ 2 - A Record of Death (1998)
❏ ❏ . . . .
❏ ❏ . . . .

BUCHANAN, Edna

Britt Montero

❏ ❏ 1 - Contents Under Pressure (1992)
❏ ❏ 2 - Miami, It's Murder (1994)☆
❏ ❏ 3 - Suitable for Framing (1995)
❏ ❏ 4 - Act of Betrayal (1996)
❏ ❏ 5 - Margin of Error (1997)
❏ ❏ . . . .
❏ ❏ . . . .

BUCKLEY, Fiona [P]

Ursula Blanchard

❏ ❏ 1 - The Robsart Mystery (1997)
❏ ❏   - U.S.-To Shield the Queen
❏ ❏ 2 - The Doublet Affair (1998)
❏ ❏ . . . .
❏ ❏ . . . .

BUCKSTAFF, Kathryn

Emily Stone

❏ ❏ 1 - No One Dies in Branson (1994)
❏ ❏ 2 - Evil Harmony (1996)
❏ ❏ . . . .
❏ ❏ . . . .

BUGGÉ, Carole

Claire Rawlings
- ❑ ❑ 1 - Who Killed Blanche Dubois (1999)
- ❑ ❑ 2 - Murder at Ravenscroft (1999)
- ❑ ❑ 3 - The Secret Drawer Society (2000)
- ❑ ❑ . . . .
- ❑ ❑ . . . .

Sherlock Holmes
- ❑ ❑ 1 - The Star of India (1998)
- ❑ ❑ . . . .
- ❑ ❑ . . . .

BURDEN, Pat

Henry Bassett
- ❑ ❑ 1 - Screaming Bones (1990)☆
- ❑ ❑ 2 - Wreath of Honesty (1990)
- ❑ ❑ 3 - Bury Him Kindly (1992)
- ❑ ❑ 4 - Father, Forgive Me (1993)
- ❑ ❑ . . . .
- ❑ ❑ . . . .

BURKE, Jan

Irene Kelly
- ❑ ❑ 1 - Goodnight, Irene (1993)☆☆
- ❑ ❑ 2 - Sweet Dreams, Irene (1994)
- ❑ ❑ 3 - Dear Irene, (1995)
- ❑ ❑ 4 - Remember Me, Irene (1996)
- ❑ ❑ 5 - Hocus (1997)☆
- ❑ ❑ 6 - Liar (1998)
- ❑ ❑ . . . .
- ❑ ❑ . . . .

BUSHELL, Agnes

Wilson & Wilder
- ❑ ❑ 1 - Shadowdance (1989)
- ❑ ❑ 2 - Death by Chrystal (1993)
- ❑ ❑ . . . .
- ❑ ❑ . . . .

BUTLER, Gwendoline
John Coffin

- ❏ ❏   1 - Dead in a Row (1957)
- ❏ ❏   2 - The Dull Dead (1958)
- ❏ ❏   3 - The Murdering Kind (1958)
- ❏ ❏   4 - Death Lives Next Door (1960)
- ❏ ❏   5 - Make Me a Murderer (1961)
- ❏ ❏   6 - Coffin in Oxford (1962)
- ❏ ❏   7 - A Coffin for Baby (1963)
- ❏ ❏   8 - Coffin Waiting (1964)
- ❏ ❏   9 - A Nameless Coffin (1966)
- ❏ ❏ 10 - Coffin Following (1968)
- ❏ ❏ 11 - Coffin's Dark Number (1969)
- ❏ ❏ 12 - A Coffin From the Past (1970)
- ❏ ❏ 13 - A Coffin for the Canary (1974)
- ❏ ❏   - U.S.-Sarsen Place
- ❏ ❏ 14 - Coffin on the Water (1986)
- ❏ ❏ 15 - Coffin in Fashion (1987)
- ❏ ❏ 16 - Coffin Underground (1988)
- ❏ ❏ 17 - Coffin in the Black Museum (1989)
- ❏ ❏ 18 - Coffin in the Museum of Crime (1989)
- ❏ ❏ 19 - Coffin and the Paper Man (1991)
- ❏ ❏ 20 - Coffin on Murder Street (1992)
- ❏ ❏ 21 - Cracking Open a Coffin (1993)
- ❏ ❏ 22 - A Coffin for Charley (1994)
- ❏ ❏ 23 - The Coffin Tree (1994)
- ❏ ❏ 24 - A Dark Coffin (1995)
- ❏ ❏ 25 - Double Coffin (1996)
- ❏ ❏ . . . .
- ❏ ❏ . . . .

BYFIELD, Barbara Ninde
Simon Bede & Helen Bullock

- ❏ ❏ 1 - Solemn High Murder [NY] (1975)
- ❏ ❏ 2 - Forever Wilt Thou Die [MI] (1976)
- ❏ ❏ 3 - A Harder Thing Than Triumph [MA] (1977)
- ❏ ❏ 4 - A Parcel of Their Fortunes [Morocco] (1979)
- ❏ ❏ . . . .
- ❏ ❏ . . . .

CAIL, Carol
Maxey Burnell
- ❏ ❏   1 - Private Lies (1993)
- ❏ ❏   2 - Unsafe Keeping (1995)
- ❏ ❏   3 - If Two of Them Are Dead (1996)
- ❏ ❏   . . . .
- ❏ ❏   . . . .

CALLOWAY, Kate
Cassidy James
- ❏ ❏   1 - First Impressions (1996)
- ❏ ❏   2 - Second Fiddle (1996)
- ❏ ❏   3 - Third Degree (1997)
- ❏ ❏   4 - Fourth Down (1998)
- ❏ ❏   5 - Fifth Wheel (1998)
- ❏ ❏   6 - Sixth Sense (1999)
- ❏ ❏   7 - Seventh Heaven (1999)
- ❏ ❏   . . . .
- ❏ ❏   . . . .

CANNELL, Dorothy
Ellie & Ben Haskell
- ❏ ❏   1 - The Thin Woman (1984)
- ❏ ❏   2 - Down the Garden Path (1985)
- ❏ ❏   3 - The Widow's Club (1988)☆☆
- ❏ ❏   4 - Mum's the Word (1990)
- ❏ ❏   5 - Femmes Fatal (1992)
- ❏ ❏   6 - How to Murder Your Mother-in-law (1994)
- ❏ ❏   7 - How to Murder the Man of Your Dreams (1995)
- ❏ ❏   8 - The Spring Cleaning Murders (1998)
- ❏ ❏   . . . .
- ❏ ❏   . . . .

CANNON, Taffy
Nan Robinson
- ❏ ❏   1 - A Pocketful of Karma (1993)
- ❏ ❏   2 - Tangled Roots (1995)
- ❏ ❏   3 - Class Reunions are Murder (1996)
- ❏ ❏   . . . .
- ❏ ❏   . . . .

CARLSON, P. M.

Bridget Mooney

❏ ❏　ss - Renowned Be Thy Grave (1998)
❏ ❏　. . . . .
❏ ❏　. . . . .

Maggie Ryan

❏ ❏　1 - Audition for Murder (1985)
❏ ❏　2 - Murder Is Academic (1985)☆
❏ ❏　3 - Murder Is Pathological (1986)
❏ ❏　4 - Murder Unrenovated (1988)☆☆
❏ ❏　5 - Rehearsal for Murder (1988)
❏ ❏　6 - Murder Misread (1990)
❏ ❏　7 - Murder in the Dog Days (1991)☆
❏ ❏　8 - Bad Blood (1991)
❏ ❏　. . . . .
❏ ❏　. . . . .

Marty LaForte Hopkins

❏ ❏　1 - Gravestone (1992)
❏ ❏　2 - Bloodstream (1995)
❏ ❏　. . . . .
❏ ❏　. . . . .

CARTER, Charlotte

Nanette Hayes

❏ ❏　1 - Rhode Island Red (1997)
❏ ❏　2 - Coq au Vin (1999)
❏ ❏　. . . . .
❏ ❏　. . . . .

CASTLE, Jayne [P]

Guinevere Jones

❏ ❏　1 - The Desperate Game (1986)
❏ ❏　2 - The Chilling Deception (1986)
❏ ❏　3 - The Sinister Touch (1986)
❏ ❏　4 - The Fatal Fortune (1986)
❏ ❏　. . . . .
❏ ❏　. . . . .

CAUDWELL, Sarah [P]
Hilary Tamar
❏ ❏   1 - Thus Was Adonis Murdered (1981)
❏ ❏   2 - The Shortest Way to Hades (1985)
❏ ❏   3 - The Sirens Sang of Murder (1989)★☆
❏ ❏   4 - The Sibyl in Her Grave (1999)
❏ ❏   . . . .
❏ ❏   . . . .

CAVERLY, Carol
Thea Barlow
❏ ❏   1 - All the Old Lions (1994)
❏ ❏   2 - Frogskin and Muttonfat (1996)
❏ ❏   . . . .
❏ ❏   . . . .

CERCONE, Karen Rose
Helen Sorby & Milo Kachigan
❏ ❏   1 - Steel Ashes (1997)
❏ ❏   2 - Blood Tracks (1998)
❏ ❏   3 - Coal Bones (1999)
❏ ❏   . . . .
❏ ❏   . . . .

CHAPMAN, Sally
Juliet Blake
❏ ❏   1 - Raw Data (1991)
❏ ❏   2 - Love Bytes (1994)
❏ ❏   3 - Cyberkiss (1996)
❏ ❏   4 - Hardwired (1997)
❏ ❏   . . . .
❏ ❏   . . . .

CHAPPELL, Helen
Holly & Sam Westcott
❏ ❏   1 - Slow Dancing With the Angel of Death (1996)
❏ ❏   2 - Dead Duck (1997)
❏ ❏   3 - Ghost of a Chance (1998)
❏ ❏   . . . .
❏ ❏   . . . .

CHARLES, Kate [P]
Lucy Kingsley & David Middleton-Brown
- ❏ ❏ 1 - A Drink of Deadly Wine (1991)
- ❏ ❏ 2 - The Snares of Death (1993)
- ❏ ❏ 3 - Appointed to Die (1994)
- ❏ ❏ 4 - A Dead Man Out of Mind (1995)
- ❏ ❏ 5 - Evil Angels Among Them (1995)
- ❏ ❏ 6 - Free Among the Dead (1997)
- ❏ ❏ 7 - Unruly Passions (1998)
- ❏ ❏ . . . .
- ❏ ❏ . . . .

CHASE, Elaine Raco
Nikki Holden & Roman Cantrell
- ❏ ❏ 1 - Dangerous Places (1987)
- ❏ ❏ 2 - Dark Corners (1988)
- ❏ ❏ . . . .
- ❏ ❏ . . . .

CHISHOLM, P. F. [P]
Robert Carey
- ❏ ❏ 1 - A Famine of Horses (1994)
- ❏ ❏ 2 - A Season of Knives (1995)
- ❏ ❏ 3 - A Surfeit of Guns (1996)
- ❏ ❏ 4 - A Plague of Angels (1998)
- ❏ ❏ . . . .
- ❏ ❏ . . . .

CHITTENDEN, Margaret
Charlie Plato
- ❏ ❏ 1 - Dying to Sing (1996)
- ❏ ❏ 2 - Dead Men Don't Dance (1997)
- ❏ ❏ 3 - Dead Beat and Deadly (1998)
- ❏ ❏ 4 - Don't Forget to Die (1999)
- ❏ ❏ . . . .
- ❏ ❏ . . . .

CHRISTMAS, Joyce

Betty Trenka

❑ ❑   1 - This Business Is Murder (1993)
❑ ❑   2 - Death at Face Value (1995)
❑ ❑   3 - Downsized to Death (1997)
❑ ❑   . . . .
❑ ❑   . . . .

Margaret Priam

❑ ❑   1 - Suddenly in Her Sorbet (1988)
❑ ❑   2 - Simply to Die For (1989)
❑ ❑   3 - A Fete Worse than Death (1990)
❑ ❑   4 - A Stunning Way to Die (1991)
❑ ❑   5 - Friend or Faux (1991)
❑ ❑   6 - It's Her Funeral (1992)
❑ ❑   7 - A Perfect Day for Dying (1994)
❑ ❑   8 - Mourning Gloria (1996)
❑ ❑   9 - Going Out in Style (1998)
❑ ❑   . . . .
❑ ❑   . . . .

CHURCHILL, Jill [P]

Jane Jeffry

❑ ❑   1 - Grime & Punishment (1989)★★☆
❑ ❑   2 - A Farewell to Yarns (1991)
❑ ❑   3 - A Quiche Before Dying (1993)
❑ ❑   4 - The Class Menagerie (1993)
❑ ❑   5 - A Knife to Remember (1994)
❑ ❑   6 - From Here to Paternity (1995)
❑ ❑   7 - Silence of the Hams (1996)
❑ ❑   8 - War and Peas (1996)
❑ ❑   9 - Fear of Frying (1997)
❑ ❑   10 - The Merchant of Menace (1998)
❑ ❑   11 - The Rite Stuff (1999)
❑ ❑   . . . .
❑ ❑   . . . .

Lily & Robert Brewster

❑ ❑   1 - Ain't Misbehavin' (1999)
❑ ❑   . . . .
❑ ❑   . . . .

CLAIRE, Edie
Leigh Koslow
❏ ❏ 1 - Never Buried (1999)
❏ ❏ 2 - Never Sorry (2000)
❏ ❏ 3 - Never Preach Past Noon (2001)
❏ ❏ . . . .
❏ ❏ . . . .

CLARK, Carol Higgins
Regan Reilly
❏ ❏ 1 - Decked (1992)☆☆
❏ ❏ 2 - Snagged (1993)
❏ ❏ 3 - Iced (1995)
❏ ❏ 4 - Twanged (1998)
❏ ❏ . . . .
❏ ❏ . . . .

CLARKE, Anna
Paula Glenning
❏ ❏ 1 - Last Judgment (1985)
❏ ❏ 2 - Cabin 3033 (1986)
❏ ❏ 3 - The Mystery Lady (1986)
❏ ❏ 4 - Last Seen in London (1987)
❏ ❏ 5 - Murder in Writing (1988)
❏ ❏ 6 - The Whitelands Affair (1989)
❏ ❏ 7 - The Case of the Paranoid Patient (1991)
❏ ❏ 8 - The Case of the Ludicrous Letters (1994)
❏ ❏ 9 - The Case of the Anxious Aunt (1996)
❏ ❏ . . . .
❏ ❏ . . . .

CLAYTON, Mary
John Reynolds
❏ ❏ 1 - Pearls Before Swine (1995)
❏ ❏ 2 - Dead Men's Bones (1996)
❏ ❏ 3 - The Prodigal's Return (1997)
❏ ❏ 4 - The Word Is Death (1997)
❏ ❏ 5 - Death Is the Inheritance (1998)
❏ ❏ . . . .
❏ ❏ . . . .

CLEARY, Melissa

Jackie Walsh & Jake

❑ ❑　1 - A Tail of Two Murders (1992)
❑ ❑　2 - Dog Collar Crime (1993)
❑ ❑　3 - Hounded to Death (1993)
❑ ❑　4 - Skull and Dog Bones (1994)
❑ ❑　5 - First Pedigree Murder (1994)
❑ ❑　6 - Dead and Buried (1994)
❑ ❑　7 - The Maltese Puppy (1995)
❑ ❑　8 - Murder Most Beastly (1996)
❑ ❑　9 - Old Dogs (1997)
❑ ❑ 10 - And Your Little Dog, Too (1998)
❑ ❑　. . . . .
❑ ❑　. . . . .

CLEEVES, Ann

George & Molly Palmer-Jones

❑ ❑　1 - A Bird in the Hand (1986)
❑ ❑　2 - Come Death and High Water (1987)
❑ ❑　3 - Murder in Paradise (1989)
❑ ❑　4 - A Prey to Murder (1989)
❑ ❑　5 - Sea Fever (1991)
❑ ❑　6 - Another Man's Poison (1992)
❑ ❑　7 - The Mill on the Shore (1994)
❑ ❑　8 - High Island Blues (1996)
❑ ❑　. . . . .
❑ ❑　. . . . .

Stephen Ramsey

❑ ❑　1 - A Lesson in Dying (1990)
❑ ❑　2 - Murder in My Backyard (1991)
❑ ❑　3 - A Day in the Death of Dorothea Cassidy (1992)
❑ ❑　4 - Killjoy (1995)
❑ ❑　5 - The Healers (1995)
❑ ❑　6 - The Baby Snatcher (1997)
❑ ❑　. . . . .
❑ ❑　. . . . .

COBURN, Laura
Kate Harrod
- ❏ ❏ 1 - A Desperate Call (1995)
- ❏ ❏ 2 - An Uncertain Death (1996)
- ❏ ❏ 3 - A Lying Silence (1997)
- ❏ ❏ . . . .
- ❏ ❏ . . . .

CODY, Liza [P]
Anna Lee
- ❏ ❏ 1 - Dupe (1980)★☆
- ❏ ❏ 2 - Bad Company (1982)
- ❏ ❏ 3 - Stalker (1984)
- ❏ ❏ 4 - Head Case (1985)
- ❏ ❏ 5 - Under Contract (1986)
- ❏ ❏ 6 - Backhand (1991)☆
- ❏ ❏ . . . .
- ❏ ❏ . . . .

Eva Wylie
- ❏ ❏ 1 - Bucket Nut (1992)★
- ❏ ❏ 2 - Monkey Wrench (1994)
- ❏ ❏ 3 - Musclebound (1997)
- ❏ ❏ . . . .
- ❏ ❏ . . . .

COEL, Margaret
John Aloysius O'Malley & Vicky Holden
- ❏ ❏ 1 - The Eagle Catcher (1995)
- ❏ ❏ 2 - The Ghost Walker (1996)
- ❏ ❏ 3 - The Dream Stalker (1997)
- ❏ ❏ 4 - The Story Teller (1998)
- ❏ ❏ . . . .
- ❏ ❏ . . . .

COGAN, Priscilla

Meggie O'Connor

- ❑ ❑   1 - Winona's Web (1997)
- ❑ ❑   2 - Compass of the Heart (1998)
- ❑ ❑   . . . .
- ❑ ❑   . . . .

COHEN, Anthea [P]

Agnes Carmichael

- ❑ ❑   1 - Angel of Vengeance (1982)
- ❑ ❑   2 - Angel Without Mercy (1982)
- ❑ ❑   3 - Angel of Death (1984)
- ❑ ❑   4 - Fallen Angel (1984)
- ❑ ❑   5 - Guardian Angel (1985)
- ❑ ❑   6 - Hell's Angel (1986)
- ❑ ❑   7 - Ministering Angel (1986)
- ❑ ❑   8 - Destroying Angel (1988)
- ❑ ❑   9 - Angel Dust (1989)
- ❑ ❑ 10 - Recording Angel (1991)
- ❑ ❑ 11 - Angel in Action (1992)
- ❑ ❑ 12 - Angel in Love (1993)
- ❑ ❑ 13 - Angel in Autumn (1995)
- ❑ ❑ 14 - Dedicated Angel (1997)
- ❑ ❑ 15 - Angel of Retribution (1998)
- ❑ ❑   . . . .
- ❑ ❑   . . . .

COKER, Carolyn

Andrea Perkins

- ❑ ❑   1 - The Other David (1984)
- ❑ ❑   2 - The Vines of Ferrara (1986)
- ❑ ❑   3 - The Hand of the Lion (1987)
- ❑ ❑   4 - The Balmoral Nude (1990)
- ❑ ❑   5 - Appearance of Evil (1993)
- ❑ ❑   . . . .
- ❑ ❑   . . . .

COLEMAN, Evelyn
Pat Conley
❏ ❏   1 - What's a Woman Gotta Do? (1998)
❏ ❏   2 - When the Gods Take a Wife (1999)
❏ ❏   . . . .
❏ ❏   . . . .

COMFORT, Barbara
Tish McWhinney
❏ ❏   1 - Phoebe's Knee (1986)
❏ ❏   2 - Grave Consequences (1989)
❏ ❏   3 - The Cashmere Kid (1993)
❏ ❏   4 - Elusive Quarry (1995)
❏ ❏   5 - A Pair for the Queen (1998)
❏ ❏   . . . .
❏ ❏   . . . .

CONANT, Susan
Holly Winter
❏ ❏   1 - A New Leash on Death (1989)
❏ ❏   2 - Dead and Doggone (1990)
❏ ❏   3 - A Bite of Death (1991)
❏ ❏   4 - Paws Before Dying (1992)
❏ ❏   5 - Gone to the Dogs (1992)
❏ ❏   6 - Bloodlines (1992)
❏ ❏   7 - Ruffly Speaking (1993)
❏ ❏   8 - Black Ribbon (1995)
❏ ❏   9 - Stud Rites (1996)
❏ ❏ 10 - Animal Appetite (1997)
❏ ❏ 11 - The Barker Street Regulars (1998)
❏ ❏   . . . .
❏ ❏   . . . .

CONNOR, Beverly
Lindsay Chamberlain
❏ ❏   1 - A Rumor of Bones (1996)
❏ ❏   2 - Questionable Remains (1997)
❏ ❏   3 - Dressed To Die (1998)
❏ ❏   . . . .
❏ ❏   . . . .

COOK, Judith
Simon Forman
- ❑ ❑ 1 - Death of a Lady's Maid (1997)
- ❑ ❑ 2 - Murder at the Rose (1998)
- ❑ ❑ . . . .
- ❑ ❑ . . . .

COOPER, Natasha [P]
Trish Maguire
- ❑ ❑ 1 - Creeping Ivy (1998)
- ❑ ❑ . . . .
- ❑ ❑ . . . .

Willow King
- ❑ ❑ 1 - Festering Lilies (1990)
- ❑ ❑   - U.S.-A Common Death
- ❑ ❑ 2 - Poison Flowers (1991)
- ❑ ❑ 3 - Bloody Roses (1992)
- ❑ ❑ 4 - Bitter Herbs (1993)
- ❑ ❑ 5 - Rotten Apples (1995)
- ❑ ❑ 6 - Fruiting Bodies (1996)
- ❑ ❑ 7 - Sour Grapes (1997)
- ❑ ❑ . . . .
- ❑ ❑ . . . .

COOPER, Susan Rogers
E. J. Pugh
- ❑ ❑ 1 - One, Two, What Did Daddy Do? (1992)
- ❑ ❑ 2 - Hickory, Dickory Stalk (1996)
- ❑ ❑ 3 - Home Again, Home Again (1997)☆
- ❑ ❑ 4 - There Was a Little Girl (1998)
- ❑ ❑ 5 - A Crooked Little House (1999)
- ❑ ❑ . . . .
- ❑ ❑ . . . .

Kimmey Kruse
- ❑ ❑ 1 - Funny as a Dead Comic (1993)
- ❑ ❑ 2 - Funny as a Dead Relative (1994)
- ❑ ❑ . . . .
- ❑ ❑ . . . .

Milton Kovak

- ❏ ❏ 1 - The Man in the Green Chevy (1988)
- ❏ ❏ 2 - Houston in the Rear View Mirror (1990)
- ❏ ❏ 3 - Other People's Houses (1990)
- ❏ ❏ 4 - Chasing Away the Devil (1991)
- ❏ ❏ 5 - Dead Moon on the Rise (1994)
- ❏ ❏ 6 - Doctors and Lawyers and Such (1995)
- ❏ ❏ . . . .
- ❏ ❏ . . . .

CORNWELL, Patricia

Andy Brazil

- ❏ ❏ 1 - Hornet's Nest (1997)
- ❏ ❏ 2 - Southern Cross (1999)
- ❏ ❏ . . . .
- ❏ ❏ . . . .

Kay Scarpetta

- ❏ ❏ 1 - Postmortem (1990)★★★★
- ❏ ❏ 2 - Body of Evidence (1991)
- ❏ ❏ 3 - All That Remains (1992)
- ❏ ❏ 4 - Cruel and Unusual (1993)★
- ❏ ❏ 5 - The Body Farm (1994)
- ❏ ❏ 6 - From Potter's Field (1995)
- ❏ ❏ 7 - Cause of Death (1996)
- ❏ ❏ 8 - Unnatural Exposure (1997)
- ❏ ❏ 9 - Point of Origin (1998)
- ❏ ❏ . . . .
- ❏ ❏ . . . .

CORPI, Lucha

new

Gloria Damasco

- ❏ ❏ 1 - Eulogy for a Brown Angel (1992)
- ❏ ❏ 2 - Cactus Blood (1995)
- ❏ ❏ . . . .
- ❏ ❏ . . . .

CRAIG, Alisa [P]

Dittany Henbit Monk & Osbert Monk

❑ ❑   1 - The Grub-and-Stakers Move a Mountain (1981)
❑ ❑   2 - The Grub-and-Stakers Quilt a Bee (1985)
❑ ❑   3 - The Grub-and-Stakers Pinch a Poke (1988)
❑ ❑   4 - The Grub-and-Stakers Spin a Yarn (1990)
❑ ❑   5 - The Grub-and-Stakers House a Haunt (1993)
❑ ❑   . . . .
❑ ❑   . . . .

Madoc & Janet Rhys

❑ ❑   1 - A Pint of Murder (1980)
❑ ❑   2 - Murder Goes Mumming (1981)
❑ ❑   3 - A Dismal Thing To Do (1986)
❑ ❑   4 - Trouble in the Brasses (1989)
❑ ❑   5 - The Wrong Rite (1992)
❑ ❑   . . . .
❑ ❑   . . . .

CRAMER, Rebecca

Linda Bluenight

❑ ❑   1 - Mission to Sonora (1998)
❑ ❑   2 - View From Frog Mountain (1999)
❑ ❑   . . . .
❑ ❑   . . . .

CRANE, Hamilton [P]

Emily D. Seeton

❑ ❑   1 - Picture Miss Seeton (1968)☆
❑ ❑   2 - Miss Seeton Draws the Line (1969)
❑ ❑   3 - Witch Miss Seeton (1971)
❑ ❑   - Brit.-Miss Seeton, Bewitched
❑ ❑   4 - Miss Seeton Sings (1973)
❑ ❑   5 - Odds on Miss Seeton (1975)
❑ ❑   6 - Miss Seeton, by Appointment
          [Hampton Charles] (1990)
❑ ❑   7 - Advantage Miss Seeton
          [Hampton Charles] (1990)
❑ ❑   8 - Miss Seeton at the Helm
          [Hampton Charles] (1990)

❑ ❑   9 - Miss Seeton Cracks the Case (1991)
❑ ❑ 10 - Miss Seeton Paints the Town (1991)
❑ ❑ 11 - Miss Seeton Rocks the Cradle (1992)
❑ ❑ 12 - Hands up, Miss Seeton (1992)
❑ ❑ 13 - Miss Seeton by Moonlight (1992)
❑ ❑ 14 - Miss Seeton Plants Suspicion (1993)
❑ ❑ 15 - Miss Seeton Goes to Bat (1993)
❑ ❑ 16 - Starring Miss Seeton (1994)
❑ ❑ 17 - Miss Seeton Undercover (1994)
❑ ❑ 18 - Miss Seeton Rules (1994)
❑ ❑ 19 - Sold to Miss Seeton (1995)
❑ ❑ 20 - Sweet Miss Seeton (1996)
❑ ❑ 21 - Bonjour, Miss Seeton (1997)
❑ ❑ 22 - Miss Seeton's Finest Hour (1999)
❑ ❑ . . . .
❑ ❑ . . . .

CRESPI, Camilla [P]
Simona Griffo

❑ ❑ 1 - The Trouble With a Small Raise (1991)
❑ ❑ 2 - The Trouble With Moonlighting (1991)
❑ ❑ 3 - The Trouble With Too Much Sun (1992)
❑ ❑ 4 - The Trouble With Thin Ice (1993)
❑ ❑ 5 - The Trouble With Going Home (1995)
❑ ❑ 6 - The Trouble With a Bad Fit (1996)
❑ ❑ 7 - The Trouble With a Bad Summer (1997)
❑ ❑ . . . .
❑ ❑ . . . .

CROMBIE, Deborah
Duncan Kincaid & Gemma James

❑ ❑ 1 - A Share in Death (1993)☆☆
❑ ❑ 2 - All Shall Be Well (1994)
❑ ❑ 3 - Leave the Grave Green (1995)
❑ ❑ 4 - Mourn Not Your Dead (1996)
❑ ❑ 5 - Dreaming of the Bones (1997)☆☆
❑ ❑ . . . .
❑ ❑ . . . .

CROSS, Amanda [P]

Kate Fansler

❏ ❏   1 - In the Last Analysis (1964)☆
❏ ❏   2 - The James Joyce Murder (1967)
❏ ❏   3 - Poetic Justice (1970)
❏ ❏   4 - The Theban Mysteries (1972)
❏ ❏   5 - The Question of Max (1976)
❏ ❏   6 - Death in a Tenured Position (1981)★
❏ ❏   - Brit.-A Death in the Faculty
❏ ❏   7 - Sweet Death, Kind Death (1984)
❏ ❏   8 - No Word From Winifred (1986)
❏ ❏   9 - A Trap for Fools (1989)
❏ ❏ 10 - The Players Come Again (1990)
❏ ❏ 11 - An Imperfect Spy (1995)
❏ ❏ ss - The Collected Stories [10 stories] (1997)
❏ ❏ 12 - The Puzzled Heart (1998)
❏ ❏   . . . .
❏ ❏   . . . .

CROWLEIGH, Ann [P]

Mirinda & Clare Clively

❏ ❏   1 - Dead as Dead Can Be (1993)
❏ ❏   2 - Wait for the Dark (1993)
❏ ❏   . . . .
❏ ❏   . . . .

CRUM, Laura

Gail McCarthy

❏ ❏   1 - Cutter (1994)
❏ ❏   2 - Hoofprints (1996)
❏ ❏   3 - Roughstock (1997)
❏ ❏   4 - Roped (1998)
❏ ❏   . . . .
❏ ❏   . . . .

CURZON, Clare [P]
Mike Yeadings
❑ ❑ 1 - I Give You Five Days (1983)
❑ ❑ 2 - Masks and Faces (1984)
❑ ❑ 3 - The Trojan Hearse (1985)
❑ ❑ 4 - The Quest for K (1986)
❑ ❑ 5 - Three-Core Lead (1988)
❑ ❑ 6 - The Blue-Eyed Boy (1990)
❑ ❑ 7 - Cat's Cradle (1992)
❑ ❑ 8 - First Wife, Twice Removed (1993)
❑ ❑ 9 - Death Prone (1994)
❑ ❑ 10 - Nice People (1995)
❑ ❑ 11 - Past Mischief (1996)
❑ ❑ 12 - Close Quarters (1997)
❑ ❑ 13 - All Unwary (1998)
❑ ❑ . . . .
❑ ❑ . . . .

CUTLER, Judith
Sophie Rivers
❑ ❑ 1 - Dying Fall (1995)
❑ ❑ 2 - Dying to Write (1996)
❑ ❑ 3 - Dying on Principle (1996)
❑ ❑ 4 - Dying for Millions (1997)
❑ ❑ 5 - Dying for Power (1998)
❑ ❑ . . . .
❑ ❑ . . . .

DAHEIM, Mary

Emma Lord

❑ ❑   1 - The Alpine Advocate (1992)☆
❑ ❑   2 - The Alpine Betrayal (1993)
❑ ❑   3 - The Alpine Christmas (1993)
❑ ❑   4 - The Alpine Decoy (1994)
❑ ❑   5 - The Alpine Escape (1995)
❑ ❑   6 - The Alpine Fury (1995)
❑ ❑   7 - The Alpine Gamble (1996)
❑ ❑   8 - The Alpine Hero (1997)
❑ ❑   9 - The Alpine Icon (1997)
❑ ❑ 10 - The Alpine Journey (1998)
❑ ❑ 11 - The Alpine Kindred (1998)
❑ ❑   . . . .
❑ ❑   . . . .

Judith McMonigle

❑ ❑   1 - Just Desserts (1991)☆
❑ ❑   2 - Fowl Prey (1991)
❑ ❑   3 - Holy Terrors (1992)
❑ ❑   4 - Dune to Death (1993)
❑ ❑   5 - Bantam of the Opera (1993)
❑ ❑   6 - Fit of Tempera (1994)
❑ ❑   7 - Major Vices (1995)
❑ ❑   8 - Murder, My Suite (1995)
❑ ❑   9 - Auntie Mayhem (1996)
❑ ❑ 10 - Nutty as a Fruitcake (1996)
❑ ❑ 11 - September Mourn (1997)
❑ ❑ 12 - Wed and Buried (1998)
❑ ❑ 13 - Snow Place To Die (1998)
❑ ❑   . . . .
❑ ❑   . . . .

DAIN, Catherine [P]

Freddie O'Neal

❑ ❑   1 - Lay It on the Line (1992)☆
❑ ❑   2 - Sing a Song of Death (1993)
❑ ❑   3 - Walk a Crooked Mile (1994)

❏ ❏   4 - Lament for a Dead Cowboy (1994)☆
❏ ❏   5 - Bet Against the House (1995)
❏ ❏   6 - The Luck of the Draw (1996)
❏ ❏   . . . .
❏ ❏   . . . .

D'AMATO, Barbara

Cat Marsala

❏ ❏   1 - Hardball (1990)
❏ ❏   2 - Hard Tack (1991)
❏ ❏   3 - Hard Luck (1992)
❏ ❏   4 - Hard Women (1993)☆
❏ ❏   5 - Hard Case (1994)
❏ ❏   6 - Hard Christmas (1995)☆☆
❏ ❏   7 - Hard Bargain (1997)
❏ ❏   . . . .
❏ ❏   . . . .

Gerritt DeGraaf

❏ ❏   1 - The Hands of Healing Murder (1980)
❏ ❏   2 - The Eyes on Utopia Murders (1981)
❏ ❏   . . . .
❏ ❏   . . . .

Suze Figueroa & Norm Bennis

❏ ❏   1 - KILLER.app (1996)
❏ ❏   2 - Good Cop, Bad Cop (1998)
❏ ❏   . . . .
❏ ❏   . . . .

DAMS, Jeanne

Dorothy Martin

❏ ❏   1 - The Body in the Transept (1995)★☆
❏ ❏   2 - Trouble in the Town Hall (1996)
❏ ❏   3 - Holy Terror in the Hebrides (1997)
❏ ❏   4 - Malice in Miniature (1998)
❏ ❏   . . . .
❏ ❏   . . . .

Hilda Johannson

❏ ❏   1 - Death in Lacquer Red (1999)
❏ ❏   2 - A Red, White and Blue Murder (2000)
❏ ❏   . . . .
❏ ❏   . . . .

DANK, Gloria

Bernard Woodrull & Snooky Randolph

❏ ❏   1 - Friends Till the End (1989)
❏ ❏   2 - Going Out in Style (1990)
❏ ❏   3 - As the Sparks Fly Upward (1992)
❏ ❏   4 - The Misfortune of Others (1993)
❏ ❏   . . . .
❏ ❏   . . . .

DANKS, Denise

Georgina Powers

❏ ❏   1 - User Deadly (1988)
❏ ❏   - Brit.-The Pizza House Crash
❏ ❏   2 - Frame Grabber (1992)
❏ ❏   3 - Wink a Hopeful Eye (1994)
❏ ❏   . . . .
❏ ❏   . . . .

DAVIDSON, Diane Mott

Goldy Bear

❏ ❏   1 - Catering to Nobody (1990)☆☆☆
❏ ❏   2 - Dying for Chocolate (1992)
❏ ❏   3 - Cereal Murders (1993)
❏ ❏   4 - The Last Suppers (1994)
❏ ❏   5 - Killer Pancake (1995)
❏ ❏   6 - The Main Corpse (1996)
❏ ❏   7 - The Grilling Season (1997)
❏ ❏   8 - Prime Cut (1998)
❏ ❏   . . . .
❏ ❏   . . . .

DAVIS, Dorothy Salisbury

Jasper Tully & Mrs. Norris

- ❏ ❏ 1 - Death of an Old Sinner (1957)
- ❏ ❏ 2 - A Gentleman Called (1958)
- ❏ ❏ 3 - Old Sinners Never Die (1959)
- ❏ ❏ . . . .
- ❏ ❏ . . . .

Julie Hayes

- ❏ ❏ 1 - A Death in the Life (1976)
- ❏ ❏ 2 - Scarlet Night (1980)
- ❏ ❏ 3 - Lullaby of Murder (1984)
- ❏ ❏ 4 - The Habit of Fear (1987)
- ❏ ❏ . . . .
- ❏ ❏ . . . .

DAVIS, Kaye

Maris Middleton

- ❏ ❏ 1 - Devil's Leg Crossing (1997)
- ❏ ❏ 2 - Possessions (1998)
- ❏ ❏ 3 - Until the End (1998)
- ❏ ❏ . . . .
- ❏ ❏ . . . .

DAVIS, Lindsey

Marcus Didius Falco

- ❏ ❏ 1 - Silver Pigs (1989)
- ❏ ❏ 2 - Shadows in Bronze (1990)
- ❏ ❏ 3 - Venus in Copper (1991)
- ❏ ❏ 4 - Iron Hand of Mars (1992)
- ❏ ❏ 5 - Poseidon's Gold (1993)☆
- ❏ ❏ 6 - Last Act in Palmyra (1994)
- ❏ ❏ 7 - Time to Depart (1995)
- ❏ ❏ 8 - A Dying Light in Corduba (1996)
- ❏ ❏ 9 - Three Hands in the Fountain (1997)
- ❏ ❏ 10 - Two for the Lions (1998)
- ❏ ❏ 11 - One Dead Virgin (1999)
- ❏ ❏ . . . .
- ❏ ❏ . . . .

DAVIS, Val [P]
Nicolette Sheridan
- ❏ ❏ 1 - Track of the Scorpion (1996)
- ❏ ❏ 2 - Flight of the Serpent (1998)
- ❏ ❏ 3 - Wake of the Hornet (1999)
- ❏ ❏ . . . .
- ❏ ❏ . . . .

DAWKINS, Cecil
Ginerva Prettifield
- ❏ ❏ 1 - The Santa Fe Rembrandt (1993)
- ❏ ❏ 2 - Rare Earth (1995)
- ❏ ❏ . . . .
- ❏ ❏ . . . .

DAWSON, Janet
Jeri Howard
- ❏ ❏ 1 - Kindred Crimes (1990)★☆☆☆
- ❏ ❏ 2 - Till the Old Men Die (1993)
- ❏ ❏ 3 - Take a Number (1993)
- ❏ ❏ 4 - Don't Turn Your Back on the Ocean (1994)
- ❏ ❏ 5 - Nobody's Child (1995)
- ❏ ❏ 6 - A Credible Threat (1996)
- ❏ ❏ 7 - Witness to Evil (1997)
- ❏ ❏ 8 - Where the Bodies Are Buried (1998)
- ❏ ❏ . . . .
- ❏ ❏ . . . .

DAY, Dianne
Fremont Jones
- ❏ ❏ 1 - The Strange Files of Fremont Jones (1995)★
- ❏ ❏ 2 - Fire and Fog (1996)
- ❏ ❏ 3 - The Bohemian Murders (1997)
- ❏ ❏ 4 - Emperor Norton's Ghost (1998)
- ❏ ❏ 5 - Death Train to Boston (1999)
- ❏ ❏ 6 - Beacon Street Mourning (2000)
- ❏ ❏ . . . .
- ❏ ❏ . . . .

DAY, Marele

Claudia Valentine

❏ ❏   1 - The Life and Crimes of Harry Lavender (1988)
❏ ❏   2 - The Case of the Chinese Boxes (1990)
❏ ❏   3 - The Last Tango of Delores Delgado (1992)★
❏ ❏   4 - The Disappearance of Madalena Grimaldi (1994)
❏ ❏   . . . .
❏ ❏   . . . .

DELOACH, Nora

Candi & Simone Covington

❏ ❏   1 - Mama Solves a Murder (1994)
❏ ❏   2 - Mama Traps a Killer (1995)
❏ ❏   3 - Mama Saves a Victim (1997)
❏ ❏   4 - Mama Stands Accused (1997)
❏ ❏   5 - Mama Stalks the Past (1997)
❏ ❏   6 - Mama Rocks the Empty Cradle (1998)
❏ ❏   . . . .
❏ ❏   . . . .

DENGLER, Sandy

Gar

❏ ❏   1 - Hyaenas (1998)
❏ ❏   2 - Wolves (2000)
❏ ❏   . . . .
❏ ❏   . . . .

Jack Prester

❏ ❏   1 - Death Valley (1993)
❏ ❏   2 - A Model Murder (1993)
❏ ❏   3 - Murder on the Mount (1994)
❏ ❏   4 - The Quick and the Dead (1995)
❏ ❏   . . . .
❏ ❏   . . . .

Joe Rodriguez

- ❏ ❏   1 - Cat Killer (1993)
- ❏ ❏   2 - Mouse Trapped (1993)
- ❏ ❏   3 - The Last Dinosaur (1994)
- ❏ ❏   4 - Gila Monster (1994)
- ❏ ❏   5 - Fatal Fishes (1995)
- ❏ ❏   . . . .
- ❏ ❏   . . . .

DENTINGER, Jane

Jocelyn O'Roarke

- ❏ ❏   1 - Murder on Cue (1983)
- ❏ ❏   2 - First Hit of the Season (1984)
- ❏ ❏   3 - Death Mask (1988)
- ❏ ❏   4 - Dead Pan (1992)
- ❏ ❏   5 - The Queen Is Dead (1994)
- ❏ ❏   6 - Who Dropped Peter Pan? (1995)
- ❏ ❏   . . . .
- ❏ ❏   . . . .

DERESKE, Jo

Helma Zukas

- ❏ ❏   1 - Miss Zukas and the Library Murders (1994)
- ❏ ❏   2 - Miss Zukas and the Island Murders (1995)
- ❏ ❏   3 - Miss Zukas and the Stroke of Death (1996)
- ❏ ❏   4 - Miss Zukas and the Raven's Dance (1996)
- ❏ ❏   5 - Out of Circulation (1997)
- ❏ ❏   6 - Final Notice (1998)
- ❏ ❏   . . . .
- ❏ ❏   . . . .

Ruby Crane

- ❏ ❏   1 - Savage Cut (1996)
- ❏ ❏   2 - Cut and Dry (1997)
- ❏ ❏   3 - Short Cut (1998)
- ❏ ❏   . . . .
- ❏ ❏   . . . .

DEWHURST, Eileen

Helen Markham

- ❏ ❏   1 - Whoever I Am (1982)
- ❏ ❏   2 - Playing Safe (1985)
- ❏ ❏   . . . .
- ❏ ❏   . . . .

Neil Carter

- ❏ ❏   1 - Curtain Fall (1977)
- ❏ ❏   2 - Drink This (1980)
- ❏ ❏   3 - Trio in Three Flats (1981)
- ❏ ❏   4 - There Was a Little Girl (1984)
- ❏ ❏   5 - A Nice Little Business (1987)
- ❏ ❏   . . . .
- ❏ ❏   . . . .

Phyllida Moon

- ❏ ❏   1 - Now You See Her (1995)
- ❏ ❏   2 - The Verdict on Winter (1996)
- ❏ ❏   . . . .
- ❏ ❏   . . . .

DIETZ, Denise

Ellie Bernstein

- ❏ ❏   1 - Throw Darts at a Cheesecake (1993)
- ❏ ❏   2 - Beat up a Cookie (1994)
- ❏ ❏   . . . .
- ❏ ❏   . . . .

DIXON, Louisa

Laura Owen

- ❏ ❏   1 - Next to Last Chance (1998)
- ❏ ❏   2 - What You Don't See (1999)
- ❏ ❏   3 - Cold Treatment (2000)
- ❏ ❏   . . . .
- ❏ ❏   . . . .

DOBSON, Joanne

Karen Pelletier

- ❏ ❏ 1 - Quieter Than Sleep (1997)☆
- ❏ ❏ 2 - The Northbury Papers (1998)
- ❏ ❏ 3 - The Raven and the Nightingale (1999)
- ❏ ❏ . . . .
- ❏ ❏ . . . .

DOMINIC, R. B. [P]

Ben Safford

- ❏ ❏ 1 - Murder Sunny Side Up (1968)
- ❏ ❏ 2 - Murder in High Place (1970)
- ❏ ❏ 3 - There is No Justice (1971)
- ❏ ❏ 4 - Epitaph for a Lobbyist (1974)
- ❏ ❏ 5 - Murder Out of Commission (1976)
- ❏ ❏ 6 - The Attending Physician (1980)
- ❏ ❏ 7 - Unexpected Developments (1984)
- ❏ ❏ . . . .
- ❏ ❏ . . . .

DONALD, Anabel

Alex Tanner

- ❏ ❏ 1 - An Uncommon Murder (1993)
- ❏ ❏ 2 - In at the Deep End (1994)
- ❏ ❏ 3 - The Glass Ceiling (1995)
- ❏ ❏ 4 - The Loop (1996)
- ❏ ❏ 5 - Destroy Unopened (1999)
- ❏ ❏ . . . .
- ❏ ❏ . . . .

DOUGLAS, Carole Nelson

Irene Adler

- ❏ ❏ 1 - Good Night, Mr. Holmes (1990)★
- ❏ ❏ 2 - Good Morning, Irene (1990)
- ❏ ❏ 3 - Irene at Large (1992)
- ❏ ❏ 4 - Irene's Last Waltz (1994)
- ❏ ❏ . . . .
- ❏ ❏ . . . .

Kevin Blake
- ❏ ❏ 1 - Probe (1985)
- ❏ ❏ 2 - Counterprobe (1990)
- ❏ ❏ . . . .
- ❏ ❏ . . . .

Temple Barr & Midnight Louie
- ❏ ❏ 1 - Catnap (1992)
- ❏ ❏ 2 - Pussyfoot (1993)
- ❏ ❏ 3 - Cat on a Blue Monday (1994)
- ❏ ❏ 4 - Cat in a Crimson Haze (1995)
- ❏ ❏ 5 - Cat in a Diamond Dazzle (1996)
- ❏ ❏ 6 - Cat With an Emerald Eye (1996)
- ❏ ❏ 7 - Cat in a Flaming Fedora (1997)
- ❏ ❏ 8 - Cat in a Golden Garland (1997)
- ❏ ❏ 9 - Cat on a Hyacinth Hunt (1998)
- ❏ ❏ . . . .
- ❏ ❏ . . . .

DOUGLAS, Lauren Wright
Allison O'Neil
- ❏ ❏ 1 - Death at Lavender Bay (1996)
- ❏ ❏ 2 - Swimming at Cat Cove (1997)
- ❏ ❏ . . . .
- ❏ ❏ . . . .

Caitlin Reece
- ❏ ❏ 1 - The Always Anonymous Beast (1987)
- ❏ ❏ 2 - Ninth Life (1989)
- ❏ ❏ 3 - The Daughters of Artemis (1991)
- ❏ ❏ 4 - A Tiger's Heart (1992)
- ❏ ❏ 5 - Goblin Market (1993)
- ❏ ❏ 6 - A Rage of Maidens (1994)
- ❏ ❏ . . . .
- ❏ ❏ . . . .

DRAKE, Alison [P]

Aline Scott

❏ ❏   1 - Tango Key (1988)
❏ ❏   2 - Fevered (1988)
❏ ❏   3 - Black Moon (1989)
❏ ❏   4 - High Strangeness (1992)
❏ ❏   . . . .
❏ ❏   . . . .

DREHER, Sarah

Stoner McTavish

❏ ❏   1 - Stoner McTavish (1985)
❏ ❏   2 - Something Shady (1986)
❏ ❏   3 - Gray Magic (1987)
❏ ❏   4 - A Captive in Time (1990)
❏ ❏   5 - Otherworld (1993)
❏ ❏   6 - Bad Company (1995)
❏ ❏   7 - Shaman's Moon (1998)
❏ ❏   . . . .
❏ ❏   . . . .

DREYER, Eileen

Molly Burke

❏ ❏   1 - Bad Medicine (1995)☆
❏ ❏   2 - Bad Reaction (2000)
❏ ❏   . . . .
❏ ❏   . . . .

DRURY, Joan M.

Tyler Jones

❏ ❏   1 - The Other Side of Silence (1993)
❏ ❏   2 - Silent Words (1996)
❏ ❏   3 - Closed in Silence (1998)
❏ ❏   . . . .
❏ ❏   . . . .

DUFFY, Margaret

Ingrid Langley & Patrick Gillard

- ❏ ❏ 1 - A Murder of Crows (1987)
- ❏ ❏ 2 - Death of a Raven (1988)
- ❏ ❏ 3 - Brass Eagle (1989)
- ❏ ❏ 4 - Who Killed Cock Robin? (1990)
- ❏ ❏ 5 - Rook-Shoot (1991)
- ❏ ❏ 6 - Gallows Bird (1993)
- ❏ ❏ . . . .
- ❏ ❏ . . . .

Joanna MacKenzie & James Carrick

- ❏ ❏ 1 - Dressed to Kill (1994)
- ❏ ❏ 2 - Prospect of Death [incl Patrick Gillard] (1995)
- ❏ ❏ 3 - Music in the Blood (1997)
- ❏ ❏ . . . .
- ❏ ❏ . . . .

DUFFY, Stella

Saz Martin

- ❏ ❏ 1 - Calendar Girl (1995)
- ❏ ❏ 2 - Wavewalker (1996)
- ❏ ❏ 3 - Beneath the Blonde (1997)
- ❏ ❏ . . . .
- ❏ ❏ . . . .

DUNANT, Sarah

Hannah Wolfe

- ❏ ❏ 1 - Birth Marks (1992)
- ❏ ❏ 2 - Fatlands (1993)★
- ❏ ❏ 3 - Under My Skin (1995)
- ❏ ❏ . . . .
- ❏ ❏ . . . .

DUNBAR, Sophie [P]

Claire Claiborne

- ❏ ❏ 1 - Behind Eclaire's Doors (1993)
- ❏ ❏ 2 - A Bad Hair Day (1996)
- ❏ ❏ 3 - Redneck Riviera (1998)

❏ ❏   4 - Shiveree (1999)
❏ ❏   5 - Senseless Ax of Beauty (2000)
❏ ❏   . . . .
❏ ❏   . . . .

DUNLAP, Susan
Jill Smith
❏ ❏   1 - Karma (1981)
❏ ❏   2 - As a Favor (1984)
❏ ❏   3 - Not Exactly a Brahmin (1985)
❏ ❏   4 - Too Close to the Edge (1987)
❏ ❏   5 - A Dinner to Die For (1987)
❏ ❏   6 - Diamond in the Buff (1990)
❏ ❏   7 - Death and Taxes (1992)
❏ ❏   8 - Time Expired (1993)
❏ ❏   9 - Sudden Exposure (1996)
❏ ❏ 10 - Cop Out (1997)
❏ ❏   . . . .
❏ ❏   . . . .

Kiernan O'Shaughnessy
❏ ❏   1 - Pious Deception (1989)☆
❏ ❏   2 - Rogue Wave (1991)☆
❏ ❏   3 - High Fall (1994)
❏ ❏   4 - No Immunity (1998)
❏ ❏   . . . .
❏ ❏   . . . .

Vejay Haskell
❏ ❏   1 - An Equal Opportunity Death (1983)
❏ ❏   2 - The Bohemian Connection (1985)
❏ ❏   3 - The Last Annual Slugfest (1986)
❏ ❏   . . . .
❏ ❏   . . . .

DUNN, Carola
Daisy Dalrymple
❏ ❏   1 - Death at Wentwater Court (1994)
❏ ❏   2 - The Winter Garden Mystery (1995)
❏ ❏   3 - Requiem for a Mezzo (1996)
❏ ❏   4 - Murder on the Flying Scotsman (1997)

❏ ❏   5 - Damsel in Distress (1997)
❏ ❏   6 - Dead in the Water (1998)
❏ ❏   . . . .
❏ ❏   . . . .

DUNNETT, Dorothy [P]
Johnson Johnson

❏ ❏   1 - The Photogenic Soprano (1968)
❏ ❏   - Brit.-Dolly and the Singing Bird
❏ ❏   2 - Murder in the Round (1970)
❏ ❏   - Brit.-Dolly and the Cookie Bird
❏ ❏   3 - Match for a Murderer (1971)
❏ ❏   - Brit.-Dolly and the Doctor Bird
❏ ❏   4 - Murder in Focus (1972)
❏ ❏   - Brit.-Dolly and the Starry Bird
❏ ❏   5 - Split Code (1976)
❏ ❏   - Brit.-Dolly and the Nanny Bird
❏ ❏   6 - Tropical Issue (1983)
❏ ❏   - Brit.-Dolly and the Bird of Paradise
❏ ❏   7 - Moroccan Traffic (1992)
❏ ❏   - Brit.-Send a Fax to the Kasbah
❏ ❏   . . . .
❏ ❏   . . . .

DYMMOCH, Michael Allen [P]
John Thinnes & Jack Caleb

❏ ❏   1 - The Man Who Understood Cats (1993)★
❏ ❏   2 - The Death of Blue Mountain Cat (1995)
❏ ❏   3 - Incendiary Designs (1998)
❏ ❏   . . . .
❏ ❏   . . . .

ECCLES, Marjorie

Gil Mayo

❑ ❑ 1 - Cast a Cold Eye (1988)
❑ ❑ 2 - Death of a Good Woman (1989)
❑ ❑ 3 - Requiem for a Dove (1990)
❑ ❑ 4 - More Deaths Than One (1990)
❑ ❑ 5 - Late of This Parish (1992)
❑ ❑ 6 - The Company She Kept (1993)
❑ ❑ 7 - An Accidental Shroud (1994)
❑ ❑ 8 - A Death of Distinction (1995)
❑ ❑ 9 - A Species of Revenge (1996)
❑ ❑ 10 - Killing Me Softly (1998)
❑ ❑   . . . .
❑ ❑   . . . .

EDGHILL, Rosemary [P]

Karen Hightower aka Bast

❑ ❑ 1 - Speak Daggers to Her (1994)
❑ ❑ 2 - Book of Moons (1995)
❑ ❑ 3 - The Bowl of Night (1996)
❑ ❑   . . . .
❑ ❑   . . . .

EDWARDS, Grace

Mali Anderson

❑ ❑ 1 - If I Should Die (1997)
❑ ❑ 2 - A Toast Before Dying (1998)
❑ ❑   . . . .
❑ ❑   . . . .

EDWARDS, Ruth Dudley

James Milton & Robert Amiss

❑ ❑ 1 - Corridors of Death (1981)☆
❑ ❑ 2 - St. Valentine's Day Murders (1985)
❑ ❑ 3 - The English School of Murder (1990)
❑ ❑   -APA-The School of English Murder
❑ ❑ 4 - Clubbed to Death (1992)☆
❑ ❑ 5 - Matricide at St. Martha's (1994)

❏ ❏ 6 - Ten Lords A-Leaping (1996)☆
❏ ❏ 7 - Murder in a Cathedral (1996)
❏ ❏ 8 - Publish and Be Murdered (1998)
❏ ❏   ....
❏ ❏   ....

EICHLER, Selma

Desiree Shapiro

❏ ❏ 1 - Murder Can Kill Your Social Life (1994)
❏ ❏ 2 - Murder Can Ruin Your Looks (1995)
❏ ❏ 3 - Murder Can Stunt Your Growth (1996)
❏ ❏ 4 - Murder Can Wreck Your Reunion (1997)
❏ ❏ 5 - Murder Can Spook Your Cat (1998)
❏ ❏ 6 - Murder Can Singe Your Old Flame (1999)
❏ ❏   ....
❏ ❏   ....

ELKINS, Charlotte & Aaron

Lee Ofsted & Graham Sheldon

❏ ❏ 1 - A Wicked Slice (1989)
❏ ❏ 2 - Rotten Lies (1995)
❏ ❏ 3 - Nasty Breaks (1997)
❏ ❏   ....
❏ ❏   ....

ELROD, P. N.

Jack Fleming

❏ ❏ 1 - Bloodlust (1990)
❏ ❏ 2 - Lifeblood (1990)
❏ ❏ 3 - Bloodcircle (1990)
❏ ❏ 4 - Art in the Blood (1991)
❏ ❏ 5 - Fire in the Blood (1991)
❏ ❏ 6 - Blood on the Water (1992)
❏ ❏ 7 - A Chill in the Blood (1998)
❏ ❏   ....
❏ ❏   ....

EMERSON, Kathy Lynn

Susanna Appleton

❏ ❏   1 - Face Down in the Marrow-Bone Pie (1997)
❏ ❏   2 - Face Down Upon an Herbal (1998)
❏ ❏   3 - Face Down Among the Winchester Geese (1999)
❏ ❏   4 - Face Down Beneath the Eleanor Cross (2000)
❏ ❏   . . . .
❏ ❏   . . . .

ENGLISH, Brenda

Sutton McPhee

❏ ❏   1 - Corruption of Faith (1997)
❏ ❏   2 - Corruption of Power (1998)
❏ ❏   . . . .
❏ ❏   . . . .

ENNIS, Catherine

Bernadette Hebert

❏ ❏   1 - Clearwater (1991)
❏ ❏   2 - Chatauqua (1993)
❏ ❏   . . . .
❏ ❏   . . . .

EPSTEIN, Carole

Barbara Simons

❏ ❏   1 - Perilous Friends (1996)
❏ ❏   2 - Perilous Relations (1997)
❏ ❏   3 - Perilous Consequences (1998)
❏ ❏   . . . .
❏ ❏   . . . .

EVANOVICH, Janet

Stephanie Plum

❏ ❏   1 - One for the Money (1994)★☆☆☆
❏ ❏   2 - Two for the Dough (1996)★
❏ ❏   3 - Three to Get Deadly (1997)★
❏ ❏   4 - Four to Score (1998)
❏ ❏   . . . .
❏ ❏   . . . .

EVANS, Geraldine

Joseph Rafferty & Dafyd Llewellyn

- ❑ ❑ 1 - Dead Before Morning (1995)
- ❑ ❑ 2 - Down Among the Dead Men (1996)
- ❑ ❑ . . . .
- ❑ ❑ . . . .

EYRE, Elizabeth [P]

Sigismondo

- ❑ ❑ 1 - Death of a Duchess (1992)
- ❑ ❑ 2 - Curtains for the Cardinal (1993)
- ❑ ❑ 3 - Poison for the Prince (1994)
- ❑ ❑ 4 - Bravo for the Bride (1994)
- ❑ ❑ 5 - Axe for an Abbot (1996)
- ❑ ❑ 6 - Dirge for a Doge (1997)
- ❑ ❑ . . . .
- ❑ ❑ . . . .

FAIRSTEIN, Linda

Alexandra Cooper

❑ ❑   1 - Final Jeopardy (1996)☆
❑ ❑   2 - Likely To Die (1997)
❑ ❑   3 - Cold Hit (1999)
❑ ❑   . . . .
❑ ❑   . . . .

FALLON, Ann C.

James Fleming

❑ ❑   1 - Blood Is Thicker (1990)
❑ ❑   2 - Where Death Lies (1991)
❑ ❑   3 - Dead Ends (1992)
❑ ❑   4 - Potter's Field (1993)
❑ ❑   5 - Hour of Our Death (1995)
❑ ❑   . . . .
❑ ❑   . . . .

FARMER, Jerrilyn

Madeline Bean

❑ ❑   1 - Sympathy for the Devil (1998)
❑ ❑   2 - Murder Hymn (1999)
❑ ❑   . . . .
❑ ❑   . . . .

FARRELL, Gillian B.

Annie McGrogan

❑ ❑   1 - Alibi for an Actress (1992)
❑ ❑   2 - Murder and a Muse (1994)
❑ ❑   . . . .
❑ ❑   . . . .

FARRELLY, Gail

Lisa King

❑ ❑   1 - Beaned in Boston (1995)
❑ ❑   2 - Duped by Derivatives (1998)
❑ ❑   . . . .
❑ ❑   . . . .

FAWCETT, Quinn [P]

Mycroft Holmes

- ❏ ❏   1 - The Adventures of Mycroft Holmes (1994)
- ❏ ❏   2 - Against the Brotherhood (1997)
- ❏ ❏   3 - Embassy Row (1998)
- ❏ ❏   . . . .
- ❏ ❏   . . . .

Victoire Vernet

- ❏ ❏   1 - Napoleon Must Die (1993)
- ❏ ❏   2 - Death Wears a Crown (1993)
- ❏ ❏   . . . .
- ❏ ❏   . . . .

FEDDERSEN, Connie

Amanda Hazard

- ❏ ❏   1 - Dead in the Water (1993)
- ❏ ❏   2 - Dead in the Cellar (1994)
- ❏ ❏   3 - Dead in the Melon Patch (1995)
- ❏ ❏   4 - Dead in the Dirt (1996)
- ❏ ❏   5 - Dead in the Mud (1997)
- ❏ ❏   6 - Dead in the Driver's Seat (1998)
- ❏ ❏   . . . .
- ❏ ❏   . . . .

FEMLING, Jean

Martha Brant

- ❏ ❏   1 - Hush, Money (1989)
- ❏ ❏   2 - Getting Mine (1991)
- ❏ ❏   . . . .
- ❏ ❏   . . . .

FENNELLY, Tony

Margo Fortier

- ❏ ❏   1 - The Hippie in the Wall (1994)
- ❏ ❏   2 - 1-900-DEAD (1997)
- ❏ ❏   . . . .
- ❏ ❏   . . . .

Matthew Arthur Sinclair

❏ ❏   1 - The Glory Hole Murders (1985)☆
❏ ❏   2 - The Closet Hanging (1987)
❏ ❏   3 - Kiss Yourself Goodbye (1989)
❏ ❏   . . . .
❏ ❏   . . . .

FERGUSON, Frances

Jane Perry

❏ ❏   1 - Missing Person (1994)
❏ ❏   2 - No Fixed Abode (1995)
❏ ❏   3 - Identity Unknown (1995)
❏ ❏   4 - With Intent to Kill (1996)
❏ ❏   . . . .
❏ ❏   . . . .

FERRIS, Monica [P]

Betsy Devonshire

❏ ❏   1 - Crewel World (1999)
❏ ❏   2 - Framed in Lace (1999)
❏ ❏   . . . .
❏ ❏   . . . .

FICKLING, G. G. [P]

Erik March

❏ ❏   1 - Naughty But Dead (1962)
❏ ❏   2 - The Case of the Radioactive Redhead (1963)
❏ ❏   3 - The Crazy Mixed-Up Nude (1964)
❏ ❏   . . . .
❏ ❏   . . . .

Honey West

❏ ❏   1 - This Girl for Hire [includes Erik March] (1957)
❏ ❏   2 - Girl on the Loose (1958)
❏ ❏   3 - A Gun for Honey (1958)
❏ ❏   4 - Girl on the Prowl (1959)
❏ ❏   5 - Honey in the Flesh (1959)
❏ ❏   6 - Dig a Dead Doll (1960)
❏ ❏   7 - Kiss for a Killer (1960)
❏ ❏   8 - Blood and Honey (1961)

❏ ❏   9 - Bombshell (1964)
❏ ❏ 10 - Honey on Her Tail (1971)
❏ ❏ 11 - Stiff as a Broad [includes Erik March] (1972)
❏ ❏   . . . .
❏ ❏   . . . .

FIEDLER, Jacqueline

Caroline Canfield

❏ ❏   1 - Tiger's Palette (1998)
❏ ❏   2 - Sketches With Wolves (1999)
❏ ❏   3 - Batscape (2000)
❏ ❏   . . . .
❏ ❏   . . . .

FITZWATER, Judy

Jennifer Marsh

❏ ❏   1 - Dying To Get Published (1998)
❏ ❏   2 - Dying To Get Even (1999)
❏ ❏   . . . .
❏ ❏   . . . .

FLETCHER, Jessica
and Donald Bain

Jessica Fletcher

❏ ❏   1 - Manhattans & Murder (1994)
❏ ❏   2 - Rum & Razors (1995)
❏ ❏   3 - Martinis & Mayhem (1995)
❏ ❏   4 - A Deadly Judgment (1996)
❏ ❏   5 - A Palette for Murder (1996)
❏ ❏   6 - The Highland Fling Murders (1997)
❏ ❏   7 - Brandy & Bullets (1997)
❏ ❏   8 - Murder on the QE2 (1997)
❏ ❏   9 - Murder in Moscow (1998)
❏ ❏   . . . .
❏ ❏   . . . .

FLORA, Kate Clark

Thea Kozak

- ❏ ❏   1 - Chosen for Death (1994)
- ❏ ❏   2 - Death in a Funhouse Mirror (1995)
- ❏ ❏   3 - Death at the Wheel (1996)
- ❏ ❏   4 - An Educated Death (1997)
- ❏ ❏   5 - Death in Paradise (1998)
- ❏ ❏   . . . .
- ❏ ❏   . . . .

FORREST, Katherine V.

Kate Delafield

- ❏ ❏   1 - Amateur City (1984)
- ❏ ❏   2 - Murder at the Nightwood Bar (1986)
- ❏ ❏   3 - The Beverly Malibu (1989)★
- ❏ ❏   4 - Murder by Tradition (1991)★
- ❏ ❏   5 - Liberty Square (1996)
- ❏ ❏   6 - Apparition Alley (1997)
- ❏ ❏   . . . .
- ❏ ❏   . . . .

FOWLER, Earlene

Benni Harper

- ❏ ❏   1 - Fool's Puzzle (1994)☆
- ❏ ❏   2 - Irish Chain (1995)
- ❏ ❏   3 - Kansas Troubles (1996)☆
- ❏ ❏   4 - Goose in the Pond (1997)☆
- ❏ ❏   5 - Dove in the Window (1998)
- ❏ ❏   6 - Mariner's Compass (1999)
- ❏ ❏   7 - Seven Sisters (2000)
- ❏ ❏   . . . .
- ❏ ❏   . . . .

FRANKEL, Valerie

Wanda Mallory

- ❏ ❏   1 - A Deadline for Murder (1991)
- ❏ ❏   2 - Murder on Wheels (1992)
- ❏ ❏   3 - Prime Time for Murder (1994)
- ❏ ❏   4 - A Body to Die For (1995)
- ❏ ❏   . . . .
- ❏ ❏   . . . .

FRASER, Anthea

David Webb

- ❑ ❑ 1 - A Shroud for Delilah (1984)
- ❑ ❑ 2 - A Necessary End (1985)
- ❑ ❑ 3 - Pretty Maids All in a Row (1986)
- ❑ ❑ 4 - Death Speaks Softly (1987)
- ❑ ❑ 5 - The Nine Bright Shiners (1987)
- ❑ ❑ 6 - Six Proud Walkers (1988)
- ❑ ❑ 7 - The April Rainers (1989)
- ❑ ❑ 8 - Symbols at Your Door (1990)
- ❑ ❑ 9 - The Lily-White Boys (1991)
- ❑ ❑ 10 - Three, Three the Rivals (1992)
- ❑ ❑ 11 - The Gospel Makers (1994)
- ❑ ❑ 12 - The Seven Stars (1995)
- ❑ ❑ 13 - One Is One and All Alone (1996)
- ❑ ❑ 14 - The Ten Commandments (1997)
- ❑ ❑ ....
- ❑ ❑ ....

FRASER, Antonia

Jemima Shore

- ❑ ❑ 1 - Quiet as a Nun (1977)
- ❑ ❑ 2 - The Wild Island (1978)
- ❑ ❑ 3 - A Splash of Red (1981)
- ❑ ❑ 4 - Cool Repentance (1982)
- ❑ ❑ 5 - Oxford Blood (1985)
- ❑ ❑ ss - Jemima Shore's First Case & Other Stories (1986)
- ❑ ❑ 6 - Your Royal Hostage (1987)
- ❑ ❑ 7 - The Cavalier Case (1991)
- ❑ ❑ ss - Jemima Shore at the Sunny Grave [9 stories] (1993)
- ❑ ❑ 8 - Political Death (1994)
- ❑ ❑ ....
- ❑ ❑ ....

FRAZER, Margaret [P]

Frevisse, Sister

- ❏ ❏   1 - The Novice's Tale (1992)
- ❏ ❏   2 - The Servant's Tale (1993)☆
- ❏ ❏   3 - The Outlaw's Tale (1994)
- ❏ ❏   4 - The Bishop's Tale (1994)
- ❏ ❏   5 - The Boy's Tale (1995)
- ❏ ❏   6 - The Murderer's Tale (1996)
- ❏ ❏   7 - The Prioress' Tale (1997)☆
- ❏ ❏   . . . .
- ❏ ❏   . . . .

FRENCH, Linda

Teddy Morelli

- ❏ ❏   1 - Talking Rain (1998)
- ❏ ❏   2 - Coffee To Die For (1998)
- ❏ ❏   3 - The Pig War (1999)
- ❏ ❏   . . . .
- ❏ ❏   . . . .

FRIEDMAN, Mickey

Georgia Lee Maxwell

- ❏ ❏   1 - Magic Mirror (1988)
- ❏ ❏   -Brit.-Deadly Reflections
- ❏ ❏   2 - A Temporary Ghost (1989)
- ❏ ❏   . . . .
- ❏ ❏   . . . .

FRITCHLEY, Alma

Letty Campbell

- ❏ ❏   1 - Chicken Run (1997)
- ❏ ❏   2 - Chicken Feed (1998)
- ❏ ❏   3 - Chicken Out (1999)
- ❏ ❏   . . . .
- ❏ ❏   . . . .

FROMER, Margot J.

Amanda Knight

- ❏ ❏ 1 - Scalpel's Edge (1991)
- ❏ ❏ 2 - Night Shift (1993)
- ❏ ❏ . . . .
- ❏ ❏ . . . .

FROMMER, Sara Hoskinson

Joan Spencer

- ❏ ❏ 1 - Murder in C Major (1986)
- ❏ ❏ 2 - Buried in Quilts (1994)
- ❏ ❏ 3 - Murder & Sullivan (1997)
- ❏ ❏ . . . .
- ❏ ❏ . . . .

FULTON, Eileen

Nina McFall & Dino Rossi

- ❏ ❏ 1 - Take One for Murder (1988)
- ❏ ❏ 2 - Death of a Golden Girl (1988)
- ❏ ❏ 3 - Dying for Stardom (1988)
- ❏ ❏ 4 - Lights, Camera, Death (1988)
- ❏ ❏ 5 - A Setting for Murder (1988)
- ❏ ❏ 6 - Fatal Flashback (1989)
- ❏ ❏ . . . .
- ❏ ❏ . . . .

FURIE, Ruthe

Fran Kirk

- ❏ ❏ 1 - If Looks Could Kill (1995)☆
- ❏ ❏ 2 - Natural Death (1996)☆
- ❏ ❏ 3 - A Deadly Pate (1996)
- ❏ ❏ . . . .
- ❏ ❏ . . . .

FYFIELD, Frances [P]

Helen West

- ❏ ❏ 1 - A Question of Guilt (1988)☆☆☆
- ❏ ❏ 2 - Trial by Fire (1990)
- ❏ ❏   - U.S.-Not That Kind of Place

❑ ❑   3 - Deep Sleep (1991)★
❑ ❑   4 - Shadow Play (1993)
❑ ❑   5 - A Clear Conscience (1994)
❑ ❑   6 - Without Consent (1996)
❑ ❑   . . . .
❑ ❑   . . . .

Sarah Fortune

❑ ❑   1 - Shadows on the Mirror (1989)
❑ ❑   2 - Perfectly Pure and Good (1994)
❑ ❑   . . . .
❑ ❑   . . . .

GALLISON, Kate
Lavinia Grey
- ❏ ❏ 1 - Bury the Bishop (1995)
- ❏ ❏ 2 - Devil's Workshop (1996)
- ❏ ❏ 3 - Unholy Angels (1996)
- ❏ ❏ 4 - Hasty Retreat (1997)
- ❏ ❏ 5 - Grave Misgivings (1998)
- ❏ ❏ . . . .
- ❏ ❏ . . . .

Nick Magaracz
- ❏ ❏ 1 - Unbalanced Accounts (1986)
- ❏ ❏ 2 - The Death Tape (1987)
- ❏ ❏ 3 - The Jersey Monkey (1992)
- ❏ ❏ . . . .
- ❏ ❏ . . . .

GARCIA-AGUILERA, Carolina
Lupe Solano
- ❏ ❏ 1 - Bloody Waters (1996)
- ❏ ❏ 2 - Bloody Shame (1997)
- ❏ ❏ 3 - Bloody Secrets (1998)
- ❏ ❏ . . . .
- ❏ ❏ . . . .

GEASON, Susan
Syd Fish
- ❏ ❏ 1 - Shaved Fish (1993)
- ❏ ❏ 2 - Dogfish (1993)
- ❏ ❏ 3 - Sharkbait (1993)
- ❏ ❏ . . . .
- ❏ ❏ . . . .

GEORGE, Anne
Mary Alice Crane & Patricia Anne Hollowell
- ❏ ❏ 1 - Murder on a Girls' Night Out (1996)★
- ❏ ❏ 2 - Murder on a Bad Hair Day (1996)

❏ ❏   3 - Murder Runs in the Family (1997)
❏ ❏   4 - Murder Makes Waves (1997)
❏ ❏   5 - Murder Gets a Life (1998)
❏ ❏   . . . .
❏ ❏   . . . .

GEORGE, Elizabeth
Thomas Lynley & Barbara Havers

❏ ❏   1 - A Great Deliverance (1988)★★☆☆
❏ ❏   2 - Payment in Blood (1989)
❏ ❏   3 - Well-Schooled in Murder (1990)
❏ ❏   4 - A Suitable Vengeance (1991)
❏ ❏   5 - For the Sake of Elena (1992)
❏ ❏   6 - Missing Joseph (1993)
❏ ❏   7 - Playing for the Ashes (1994)
❏ ❏   8 - In the Presence of the Enemy (1996)
❏ ❏   9 - Deception on His Mind (1997)
❏ ❏   . . . .
❏ ❏   . . . .

GILL, B. M. [P]
Tom Maybridge

❏ ❏   1 - Victims (1980)
❏ ❏   - U.S.-Suspect
❏ ❏   2 - Seminar for Murder (1985)
❏ ❏   3 - The Fifth Rapunzel (1990)
❏ ❏   . . . .
❏ ❏   . . . .

GILMAN, Dorothy
Emily Pollifax

❏ ❏   1 - The Unexpected Mrs. Pollifax (1966)
❏ ❏   2 - The Amazing Mrs. Pollifax (1970)
❏ ❏   3 - The Elusive Mrs. Pollifax (1971)
❏ ❏   4 - A Palm for Mrs. Pollifax (1973)
❏ ❏   5 - Mrs. Pollifax on Safari (1976)
❏ ❏   6 - Mrs. Pollifax on the China Station (1983)
❏ ❏   7 - Mrs. Pollifax and the Hong Kong Buddha (1985)
❏ ❏   8 - Mrs. Pollifax and the Golden Triangle (1988)
❏ ❏   9 - Mrs. Pollifax and the Whirling Dervish (1990)

❏ ❏ 10 - Mrs. Pollifax and the Second Thief (1993)
❏ ❏ 11 - Mrs. Pollifax Pursued (1995)
❏ ❏ 12 - Mrs. Pollifax and the Lion Killer (1996)
❏ ❏ 13 - Mrs. Pollifax, Innocent Tourist (1997)
❏ ❏   . . . .
❏ ❏   . . . .

GILPATRICK, Noreen

Kate MacLean

❏ ❏   1 - Final Design (1993)
❏ ❏   2 - Shadow of Death (1995)
❏ ❏   . . . .
❏ ❏   . . . .

GIRDNER, Jaqueline

Kate Jasper

❏ ❏   1 - Adjusted to Death (1991)
❏ ❏   2 - The Last Resort (1991)
❏ ❏   3 - Murder Most Mellow (1992)
❏ ❏   4 - Fat-Free and Fatal (1993)
❏ ❏   5 - Tea-Totally Dead (1994)
❏ ❏   6 - A Stiff Critique (1995)
❏ ❏   7 - Most Likely to Die (1996)
❏ ❏   8 - A Cry for Self Help (1997)
❏ ❏   9 - Death Hits the Fan (1998)
❏ ❏ 10 - Murder on the Astral Plane (1999)
❏ ❏ 11 - Murder, My Deer (2000)
❏ ❏   . . . .
❏ ❏   . . . .

GIROUX, E. X. [P]

Robert Forsythe & Abigail Sanderson

❏ ❏   1 - A Death for Adonis (1984)
❏ ❏   2 - A Death for a Darling (1985)
❏ ❏   3 - A Death for a Dancer (1986)
❏ ❏   4 - A Death for a Doctor (1986)
❏ ❏   5 - A Death for a Dilletante (1987)
❏ ❏   6 - A Death for a Dietician (1988)

❏ ❏   7 - A Death for a Dreamer (1989)
❏ ❏   8 - A Death for a Double (1990)
❏ ❏   9 - A Death for a Dancing Doll (1991)
❏ ❏ 10 - A Death for a Dodo (1993)
❏ ❏   . . . .
❏ ❏   . . . .

GLASS, Leslie

April Woo

❏ ❏   1 - Burning Time (1993)
❏ ❏   2 - Hanging Time (1995)
❏ ❏   3 - Loving Time (1996)
❏ ❏   4 - Judging Time (1998)
❏ ❏   . . . .
❏ ❏   . . . .

GLEN, Alison [P]

Charlotte Sams

❏ ❏   1 - Showcase (1992)
❏ ❏   2 - Trunk Show (1995)
❏ ❏   . . . .
❏ ❏   . . . .

GODFREY, Ellen

Jane Tregar

❏ ❏   1 - Murder Behind Locked Doors (1988)
❏ ❏   2 - Georgia Disappeared (1991)
❏ ❏   . . . .
❏ ❏   . . . .

Janet Barkin

❏ ❏   1 - Murder on the Loose (1999)
❏ ❏   2 - Murder on the Lover's Bridge (1999)
❏ ❏   3 - Murder in the Shadows (1999)
❏ ❏   . . . .
❏ ❏   . . . .

Rebecca Rosenthal
❏ ❏ 1 - The Case of the Cold Murderer (1976)
❏ ❏ 2 - Murder Among the Well-to-do (1977)
❏ ❏ . . . .
❏ ❏ . . . .

GOLDSTONE, Nancy
Elizabeth Halperin
❏ ❏ 1 - Mommy and the Murder (1995)
❏ ❏ 2 - Mommy and the Money (1997)
❏ ❏ . . . .
❏ ❏ . . . .

GOM, Leona
Vicky Bauer
❏ ❏ 1 - After-Image (1998)
❏ ❏ 2 - Double Negative (1998)
❏ ❏ . . . .
❏ ❏ . . . .

GORDON, Alison
Kate Henry
❏ ❏ 1 - The Dead Pull Hitter (1989)
❏ ❏ 2 - Safe at Home (1991)
❏ ❏ 3 - Night Game (1993)
❏ ❏ 4 - Striking Out (1995)
❏ ❏ 5 - Prairie Hardball (1997)
❏ ❏ 6 - Suicide Squeeze (1999)
❏ ❏ . . . .
❏ ❏ . . . .

GOSLING, Paula
Blackwater Bay Mystery
❏ ❏ 1 - A Few Dying Words (1994)
❏ ❏ 2 - The Dead of Winter (1995)
❏ ❏ 3 - Death and Shadows (1998)
❏ ❏ . . . .
❏ ❏ . . . .

Jack Stryker & Kate Trevorne

❏ ❏   1 - Monkey Puzzle (1985)★
❏ ❏   2 - Backlash (1989)
❏ ❏   3 - The Body in Blackwater Bay (1992)
❏ ❏   . . . .
❏ ❏   . . . .

Luke Abbott

❏ ❏   1 - The Wychford Murders (1986)
❏ ❏   2 - Death Penalties (1991)
❏ ❏   . . . .
❏ ❏   . . . .

GRAFTON, Sue

Kinsey Millhone

❏ ❏   1 - "A" is for Alibi (1982)★☆
❏ ❏   2 - "B" is for Burglar (1985)★★
❏ ❏   3 - "C" is for Corpse (1986)★☆
❏ ❏   4 - "D" is for Deadbeat (1987)
❏ ❏   5 - "E" is for Evidence (1988)☆
❏ ❏   6 - "F" is for Fugitive (1989)
❏ ❏   7 - "G" is for Gumshoe (1990)★★
❏ ❏   8 - "H" is for Homicide (1991)
❏ ❏   9 - "I" is for Innocent (1992)★
❏ ❏ 10 - "J" is for Judgment (1993)
❏ ❏ 11 - "K" is for Killer (1994)★☆
❏ ❏ 12 - "L" is for Lawless (1995)
❏ ❏ 13 - "M" is for Malice (1996)
❏ ❏ 14 - "N" is for Noose (1998)
❏ ❏   . . . .
❏ ❏   . . . .

GRAHAM, Caroline

Tom Barnaby

❏ ❏   1 - The Killings at Badger's Drift (1987)★☆☆
❏ ❏   2 - Death of a Hollow Man (1989)
❏ ❏   3 - Death in Disguise (1993)
❏ ❏   4 - Written in Blood (1995)
❏ ❏   5 - Faithful Unto Death (1996)
❏ ❏   . . . .
❏ ❏   . . . .

GRANGER, Ann
Alan Markby & Meredith Mitchell
- ❑ ❑ 1 - Say It With Poison (1991)
- ❑ ❑ 2 - A Season for Murder (1992)
- ❑ ❑ 3 - Cold in the Earth (1993)
- ❑ ❑ 4 - Murder Among Us (1993)
- ❑ ❑ 5 - Where Old Bones Lie (1993)
- ❑ ❑ 6 - A Fine Place for Death (1994)
- ❑ ❑ 7 - Flowers for His Funeral (1994)
- ❑ ❑ 8 - A Candle for a Corpse (1995)
- ❑ ❑ 9 - A Touch of Mortality (1996)
- ❑ ❑ 10 - A Word After Dying (1996)
- ❑ ❑ 11 - Call the Dead Again (1998)
- ❑ ❑ . . . .
- ❑ ❑ . . . .

GRANGER, Ann
Fran Varaday
- ❑ ❑ 1 - Asking for Trouble (1997)
- ❑ ❑ 2 - Keeping Bad Company (1997)
- ❑ ❑ . . . .
- ❑ ❑ . . . .

GRANT, Anne Underwood
Sidney Teague
- ❑ ❑ 1 - Multiple Listing (1998)
- ❑ ❑ 2 - Smoke Screen (1998)
- ❑ ❑ 3 - Cuttings (1999)
- ❑ ❑ . . . .
- ❑ ❑ . . . .

GRANT, Linda [P]
Catherine Sayler
- ❑ ❑ 1 - Random Access Murder (1988)☆
- ❑ ❑ 2 - Blind Trust (1990)
- ❑ ❑ 3 - Love nor Money (1991)☆
- ❑ ❑ 4 - A Woman's Place (1994)

❏ ❏   5 - Lethal Genes (1996)☆
❏ ❏   6 - Vampire Bytes (1998)
❏ ❏   . . . .
❏ ❏   . . . .

GRANT-ADAMSON, Lesley
Jim Rush
❏ ❏   1 - A Life of Adventure (1992)
❏ ❏   2 - Dangerous Games (1994)
❏ ❏   . . . .
❏ ❏   . . . .

Rain Morgan
❏ ❏   1 - Patterns in the Dust (1985)
❏ ❏   - U.S.-Death on Widow's Walk
❏ ❏   2 - The Face of Death (1985)
❏ ❏   3 - Guilty Knowledge (1986)
❏ ❏   4 - Wild Justice (1987)
❏ ❏   5 - Curse the Darkness (1990)
❏ ❏   . . . .
❏ ❏   . . . .

GRAVES, Sarah
Jacobia Triptree
❏ ❏   1 - The Dead Cat Bounce (1998)
❏ ❏   2 - A Blond for a Shiling (1999)
❏ ❏   . . . .
❏ ❏   . . . .

GRAY, Dulcie [P]
Insp. Supt. Cardiff
❏ ❏   1 - Epitaph for a Dead Actor (1960)
❏ ❏   2 - Died in the Red (1967)
❏ ❏   . . . .
❏ ❏   . . . .

GRAY, Gallagher [P]
Theodore S. Hubbert & Auntie Lil
❏ ❏   1 - Partners in Crime (1991)
❏ ❏   2 - A Cast of Killers (1992)

❑ ❑   3 - Death of a Dream Maker (1995)
❑ ❑   4 - A Motive for Murder (1996)
❑ ❑   . . . .
❑ ❑   . . . .

GREEN, Christine

Connor O'Neill & Fran Wilson

❑ ❑   1 - Death in the Country (1994)
❑ ❑   2 - Die in My Dreams (1995)
❑ ❑   3 - Fatal Cut (1996)
❑ ❑   . . . .
❑ ❑   . . . .

Kate Kinsella

❑ ❑   1 - Deadly Errand (1991)
❑ ❑   2 - Deadly Admirer (1992)
❑ ❑   3 - Deadly Practice (1994)
❑ ❑   4 - Deadly Partners (1996)
❑ ❑   . . . .
❑ ❑   . . . .

GREEN, Edith Pinero

Dearborn V. Pinch

❑ ❑   1 - Rotten Apples (1977)
❑ ❑   2 - Sneaks (1979)
❑ ❑   3 - Perfect Fools (1982)
❑ ❑   . . . .
❑ ❑   . . . .

GREEN, Kate

Theresa Fortunato & Oliver Jardino

❑ ❑   1 - Shattered Moon (1986)☆
❑ ❑   2 - Black Dreams (1993)
❑ ❑   3 - Angel Falls (1997)
❑ ❑   . . . .
❑ ❑   . . . .

GREENWOOD, Diane M.
Theodora Braithwaite
- ❑ ❑ 1 - Clerical Errors (1991)
- ❑ ❑ 2 - Unholy Ghosts (1992)
- ❑ ❑ 3 - Idol Bones (1993)
- ❑ ❑ 4 - Holy Terrors (1994)
- ❑ ❑ 5 - Every Deadly Sin (1995)
- ❑ ❑ 6 - Mortal Spoils (1996)
- ❑ ❑ 7 - Heavenly Vices (1997)
- ❑ ❑ 8 - A Grave Disturbance (1998)
- ❑ ❑ . . . .
- ❑ ❑ . . . .

GREENWOOD, Kerry
Phryne Fisher
- ❑ ❑ 1 - Cocaine Blues (1989)
- ❑ ❑   - U.S.-Death by Misadventure
- ❑ ❑ 2 - Flying Too High (1990)
- ❑ ❑ 3 - Murder on the Ballarat Train (1991)
- ❑ ❑ 4 - Death at Victoria Dock (1992)
- ❑ ❑ 5 - The Green Mill Murder (1993)
- ❑ ❑ 6 - Blood and Circuses (1994)
- ❑ ❑ 7 - Ruddy Gore (1995)
- ❑ ❑ 8 - Urn Burial (1996)
- ❑ ❑ 9 - Ashes and Almonds (1997)
- ❑ ❑ . . . .
- ❑ ❑ . . . .

GREGORY, Susanna [P]
Matthew Bartholomew
- ❑ ❑ 1 - A Plague on Both Your Houses (1996)
- ❑ ❑ 2 - An Unholy Alliance (1996)
- ❑ ❑ 3 - A Bone of Contention (1997)
- ❑ ❑ 4 - A Deadly Brew (1998)
- ❑ ❑ . . . .
- ❑ ❑ . . . .

GRETH, Roma
Hana Shaner
- ❏ ❏ 1 - Now You Don't (1988)
- ❏ ❏ 2 - Plain Murder (1989)
- ❏ ❏ . . . .
- ❏ ❏ . . . .

GRIFFIN, Annie [P]
Hannah Malloy
- ❏ ❏ 1 - A Very Eligible Corpse (1998)
- ❏ ❏ 2 - Date With the Perfect Dead Man (1999)
- ❏ ❏ . . . .
- ❏ ❏ . . . .

GRIMES, Martha
Richard Jury
- ❏ ❏ 1 - The Man With a Load of Mischief (1981)
- ❏ ❏ 2 - The Old Fox Deceived (1982)
- ❏ ❏ 3 - The Anodyne Necklace (1983)★
- ❏ ❏ 4 - The Dirty Duck (1984)
- ❏ ❏ 5 - Jerusalem Inn (1984)
- ❏ ❏ 6 - Help the Poor Struggler (1985)
- ❏ ❏ 7 - The Deer Leap (1985)
- ❏ ❏ 8 - I Am the Only Running Footman (1986)
- ❏ ❏ 9 - The Five Bells and Bladebone (1987)
- ❏ ❏ 10 - The Old Silent (1989)
- ❏ ❏ 11 - The Old Contemptibles (1990)
- ❏ ❏ 12 - The Horse You Came in On (1993)
- ❏ ❏ 13 - Rainbow's End (1995)
- ❏ ❏ 14 - The Case Has Altered (1997)
- ❏ ❏ 15 - The Stargazey (1998)
- ❏ ❏ . . . .
- ❏ ❏ . . . .

GRIMES, Terris McMahan
Theresa Galloway
- ❏ ❏ 1 - Somebody Else's Child (1996)★★☆
- ❏ ❏ 2 - Blood Will Tell (1997)
- ❏ ❏ 3 - Other Duties As Required (1998)
- ❏ ❏ . . . .
- ❏ ❏ . . . .

GRINDLE, Lucretia

H. W. Ross

❏ ❏   1 - The Killing of Ellis Martin (1993)
❏ ❏   2 - So Little to Die For (1994)
❏ ❏   . . . .
❏ ❏   . . . .

GUIVER, Patricia

Delilah Doolittle

❏ ❏   1 - Delilah Doolittle and the Purloined Pooch (1997)
❏ ❏   2 - Delilah Doolittle and the Purloined Pooch (1998)
❏ ❏   3 - Delilah Doolittle and the Careless Coyote (1998)
❏ ❏   . . . .
❏ ❏   . . . .

GUNN, Elizabeth

Jake Hines

❏ ❏   1 - Triple Play (1997)
❏ ❏   2 - Par Four (1998)
❏ ❏   . . . .
❏ ❏   . . . .

GUNNING, Sally

Peter Bartholomew

❏ ❏   1 - Hot Water (1990)
❏ ❏   2 - Under Water (1992)
❏ ❏   3 - Ice Water (1993)
❏ ❏   4 - Troubled Water (1993)
❏ ❏   5 - Rough Water (1994)
❏ ❏   6 - Still Water (1996)
❏ ❏   7 - Muddy Water (1997)
❏ ❏   8 - Dirty Water (1998)
❏ ❏   9 - Fire Water (1999)
❏ ❏   . . . .
❏ ❏   . . . .

GUR, Batya

Michael Ohayon

❏ ❏ 1 - Saturday Morning Murder (1988)
❏ ❏ 2 - Literary Murder (1993)
❏ ❏ 3 - Murder on the Kibbutz: A Communal Case
              (1994)☆
❏ ❏ 4 - Murder Duet (1999)
❏ ❏   . . . .
❏ ❏   . . . .

HADDAD, Carolyn A.

David Haham

- ❏ ❏   1 - Bloody September (1976)
- ❏ ❏   2 - Operation Apricot (1978)
- ❏ ❏   . . . .
- ❏ ❏   . . . .

HADDAM, Jane [P]

Gregor Demarkian

- ❏ ❏   1 - Not a Creature Was Stirring (1990)☆☆
- ❏ ❏   2 - Precious Blood (1991)
- ❏ ❏   3 - Act of Darkness (1991)
- ❏ ❏   4 - Quoth the Raven (1991)
- ❏ ❏   5 - A Great Day for the Deadly (1992)
- ❏ ❏   6 - Feast of Murder (1992)
- ❏ ❏   7 - A Stillness in Bethlehem (1992)
- ❏ ❏   8 - Murder Superior (1993)
- ❏ ❏   9 - Festival of Deaths (1993)
- ❏ ❏ 10 - Bleeding Hearts (1994)
- ❏ ❏ 11 - Dear Old Dead (1994)
- ❏ ❏ 12 - Fountain of Death (1995)
- ❏ ❏ 13 - And One to Die On (1996)
- ❏ ❏ 14 - Deadly Beloved (1997)
- ❏ ❏   . . . .
- ❏ ❏   . . . .

HADDOCK, Lisa

Carmen Ramirez

- ❏ ❏   1 - Edited Out (1994)
- ❏ ❏   2 - Final Cut (1995)
- ❏ ❏   . . . .
- ❏ ❏   . . . .

HAFFNER, Margaret

Catherine Edison

- ❏ ❏   1 - A Murder of Crows (1992)
- ❏ ❏   2 - A Killing Frost (1994)
- ❏ ❏   . . . .
- ❏ ❏   . . . .

HAGER, Jean

Mitch Bushyhead

❏ ❏ 1 - The Grandfather Medicine (1989)
❏ ❏ 2 - Night Walker (1990)
❏ ❏ 3 - Ghostland (1992)
❏ ❏ 4 - The Fire Carrier (1996)
❏ ❏ 5 - Masked Dancers (1998)
❏ ❏ . . . .
❏ ❏ . . . .

Molly Bearpaw

❏ ❏ 1 - Ravenmocker (1992)
❏ ❏ 2 - The Redbird's Cry (1994)
❏ ❏ 3 - Seven Black Stones (1995)
❏ ❏ 4 - The Spirit Caller (1997)
❏ ❏ . . . .
❏ ❏ . . . .

Tess Darcy

❏ ❏ 1 - Blooming Murder (1994)
❏ ❏ 2 - Dead and Buried (1995)
❏ ❏ 3 - Death on the Drunkard's Path (1996)
❏ ❏ 4 - The Last Noel (1997)
❏ ❏ 5 - Sew Deadly (1998)
❏ ❏ . . . .
❏ ❏ . . . .

HALL, Linda

Roger Sheppard

❏ ❏ 1 - August Gamble (1995)
❏ ❏ 2 - November Veil (1996)
❏ ❏ 3 - April Operation (1997)
❏ ❏ . . . .
❏ ❏ . . . .

HALL, Patricia [P]

Laura Ackroyd & Michael Thackeray

❏ ❏ 1 - Death by Election (1993)
❏ ❏ 2 - Dying Fall (1994)
❏ ❏ 3 - In the Bleak Midwinter (1995)
❏ ❏   - U.S.-Dead of Winter

❏ ❏   4 - Perils of the Night (1997)
❏ ❏   5 - The Italian Girl (1998)
❏ ❏   . . . .
❏ ❏   . . . .

HAMBLY, Barbara

Benjamin January

❏ ❏   1 - Free Man of Color (1997)
❏ ❏   2 - Fever Season (1998)
❏ ❏   . . . .
❏ ❏   . . . .

James Asher

❏ ❏   1 - Those Who Hunt the Night (1988)
❏ ❏   2 - Traveling With the Dead (1995)
❏ ❏   . . . .
❏ ❏   . . . .

HAMILTON, Laurell K.

Anita Blake

❏ ❏   1 - Guilty Pleasures (1993)
❏ ❏   2 - The Laughing Corpse (1994)
❏ ❏   3 - Circus of the Damned (1995)
❏ ❏   4 - The Lunatic Cafe (1996)
❏ ❏   5 - Bloody Bones (1996)
❏ ❏   6 - The Killing Dance (1997)
❏ ❏   7 - Burnt Offerings (1998)
❏ ❏   . . . .
❏ ❏   . . . .

HAMILTON, Lyn

Lara McClintock

❏ ❏   1 - The Xibalba Murders [Mexico] (1997)
❏ ❏   2 - The Maltese Goddess [Malta] (1998)
❏ ❏   3 - The Moche Warrior [Peru] (1999)
❏ ❏   4 - The Amairgen Puzzle [Ireland] (2000)
❏ ❏   . . . .
❏ ❏   . . . .

HANEY, Lauren [P]

Lt. Bak

- ❏ ❏ 1 - The Right Hand of Amon (1997)
- ❏ ❏ 2 - A Face Turned Backward (1998)
- ❏ ❏ . . . .
- ❏ ❏ . . . .

HARDWICK, Mollie

Doran Fairweather

- ❏ ❏ 1 - Malice Domestic (1986)
- ❏ ❏ 2 - Parson's Pleasure (1987)
- ❏ ❏ 3 - Uneaseful Death (1988)
- ❏ ❏ 4 - The Bandersnatch (1989)
- ❏ ❏ 5 - Perish in July (1989)
- ❏ ❏ 6 - The Dreaming Damozel (1990)
- ❏ ❏ 7 - Come Away, Death (1997)
- ❏ ❏ . . . .
- ❏ ❏ . . . .

HARRIS, Charlaine

Aurora Teagarden

- ❏ ❏ 1 - Real Murders (1990)☆
- ❏ ❏ 2 - A Bone to Pick (1992)
- ❏ ❏ 3 - Three Bedrooms, One Corpse (1994)
- ❏ ❏ 4 - The Julius House (1995)
- ❏ ❏ 5 - Dead Over Heels (1996)
- ❏ ❏ 6 - A Fool and His Honey (1999)
- ❏ ❏ . . . .
- ❏ ❏ . . . .

Lily Bard

- ❏ ❏ 1 - Shakespeare's Landlord (1996)
- ❏ ❏ 2 - Shakespeare's Champion (1997)
- ❏ ❏ 3 - Shakespeare's Christmas (1998)
- ❏ ❏ . . . .
- ❏ ❏ . . . .

HARRIS, Lee [P]

Christine Bennett

❑ ❑ 1 - The Good Friday Murder (1992)☆
❑ ❑ 2 - The Yom Kippur Murder (1992)
❑ ❑ 3 - The Christening Day Murder (1993)
❑ ❑ 4 - The St. Patrick's Day Murder (1994)
❑ ❑ 5 - The Christmas Night Murder (1994)
❑ ❑ 6 - The Thanksgiving Day Murder (1995)
❑ ❑ 7 - The Passover Murder (1996)
❑ ❑ 8 - The Valentine's Day Murder (1997)
❑ ❑ 9 - The New Year's Eve Murder (1997)
❑ ❑ 10 - The Labor Day Murder (1998)
❑ ❑ 11 - The Father's Day Murder (1999)
❑ ❑ . . . .
❑ ❑ . . . .

HARRISON, Jamie

Jules Clement

❑ ❑ 1 - The Edge of the Crazies (1995)
❑ ❑ 2 - Going Local (1996)
❑ ❑ 3 - An Unfortunate Prairie Occurance (1998)
❑ ❑ . . . .
❑ ❑ . . . .

HARROD-EAGLES, Cynthia

Bill Slider

❑ ❑ 1 - Orchestrated Death (1991)
❑ ❑ 2 - Death Watch (1992)
❑ ❑ 3 - Death To Go (1993)
❑ ❑   - APA-Necrochip
❑ ❑ 4 - Grave Music (1994)
❑ ❑   - Brit.-Dead End
❑ ❑ 5 - Blood Lines (1996)
❑ ❑ 6 - Killing Time (1996)
❑ ❑ 7 - Shallow Grave (1998)
❑ ❑ . . . .
❑ ❑ . . . .

HART, Carolyn G.

Annie Laurance & Max Darling

- ❏ ❏ 1 - Death on Demand (1987)☆☆
- ❏ ❏ 2 - Design for Murder (1987)
- ❏ ❏ 3 - Something Wicked (1988)★★
- ❏ ❏ 4 - Honeymoon With Murder (1988)★
- ❏ ❏ 5 - A Little Class on Murder (1989)★☆☆
- ❏ ❏ 6 - Deadly Valentine (1990)☆☆
- ❏ ❏ 7 - The Christie Caper (1991)☆☆☆
- ❏ ❏ 8 - Southern Ghost (1992)☆☆
- ❏ ❏ 9 - The Mint Julep Murder (1995)
- ❏ ❏ 10 - Yankee Doodle Dead (1998)
- ❏ ❏ . . . .
- ❏ ❏ . . . .

Henrietta O'Dwyer Collins

- ❏ ❏ 1 - Dead Man's Island (1993)★
- ❏ ❏ 2 - Scandal in Fair Haven (1994)☆
- ❏ ❏ 3 - Death in Lovers' Lane (1997)
- ❏ ❏ 4 - Death in Paradise (1998)
- ❏ ❏ . . . .
- ❏ ❏ . . . .

HART, Ellen [P]

Jane Lawless

- ❏ ❏ 1 - Hallowed Murder (1989)
- ❏ ❏ 2 - Vital Lies (1991)
- ❏ ❏ 3 - Stage Fright (1992)
- ❏ ❏ 4 - A Killing Cure (1993)
- ❏ ❏ 5 - A Small Sacrifice (1994)★
- ❏ ❏ 6 - Faint Praise (1995)
- ❏ ❏ 7 - Robber's Wine (1996)★
- ❏ ❏ 8 - Wicked Games (1998)
- ❏ ❏ . . . .
- ❏ ❏ . . . .

Sophie Greenway

- ❏ ❏   1 - This Little Piggy Went to Murder (1994)
- ❏ ❏   2 - For Every Evil (1995)
- ❏ ❏   3 - The Oldest Sin (1996)
- ❏ ❏   4 - Murder in the Air (1997)
- ❏ ❏   . . . .
- ❏ ❏   . . . .

HARTZMARK, Gini

Katherine Prescott Milholland

- ❏ ❏   1 - Principal Defense (1992)☆
- ❏ ❏   2 - Final Option (1994)
- ❏ ❏   3 - Bitter Business (1995)
- ❏ ❏   4 - Fatal Reaction (1997)
- ❏ ❏   5 - Rough Trade (1999)
- ❏ ❏   . . . .
- ❏ ❏   . . . .

HATHAWAY, Robin

Andrew Fenimore

- ❏ ❏   1 - The Doctor Digs a Grave (1998)★
- ❏ ❏   2 - The Doctor and the Doll House (1999)
- ❏ ❏   . . . .
- ❏ ❏   . . . .

HAYDEN, G. Miki

Dennis Astin

- ❏ ❏   1 - By Reason of Insanity (1998)
- ❏ ❏   2 - Too Old for Murder (1999)
- ❏ ❏   . . . .
- ❏ ❏   . . . .

HAYMON, S. T.

Benjamin Jurnet

- ❏ ❏   1 - Death and the Pregnant Virgin (1980)
- ❏ ❏   2 - Ritual Murder (1982)★
- ❏ ❏   3 - Stately Homicide (1984)
- ❏ ❏   4 - Death of a God (1987)
- ❏ ❏   5 - A Very Particular Murder (1989)

❏ ❏   6 - Death of a Warrior Queen (1991)
❏ ❏   7 - A Beautiful Death (1993)
❏ ❏   8 - Death of a Hero (1996)
❏ ❏   . . . .
❏ ❏   . . . .

HAYTER, Sparkle

Robin Hudson

❏ ❏   1 - What's a Girl Gotta Do? (1994)★
❏ ❏   2 - Nice Girls Finish Last (1996)☆
❏ ❏   3 - Revenge of the Cootie Girls (1997)
❏ ❏   4 - The Last Manly Man (1998)
❏ ❏   . . . .
❏ ❏   . . . .

HEBDEN, Juliet [P]

Clovis Pel

❏ ❏   1 - Death Set to Music
          [by Mark Hebden] (1979)
❏ ❏   - APA-Pel and the Parked Car (1995)
❏ ❏   2 - Pel and Faceless Corpse
          [by Mark Hebden] (1979)
❏ ❏   3 - Pel Under Pressure
          [by Mark Hebden] (1980)
❏ ❏   4 - Pel is Puzzled
          [by Mark Hebden] (1981)
❏ ❏   5 - Pel and the Stagehound
          [by Mark Hebden] (1982)
❏ ❏   6 - Pel and the Bombers
          [by Mark Hebden] (1982)
❏ ❏   7 - Pel and the Predators
          [by Mark Hebden] (1984)
❏ ❏   8 - Pel and the Pirates
          [by Mark Hebden] (1984)
❏ ❏   9 - Pel and the Prowler
          [by Mark Hebden] (1985)
❏ ❏ 10 - Pel and the Paris Mob
          [by Mark Hebden] (1986)
❏ ❏ 11 - Pel Among the Pueblos
          [by Mark Hebden] (1987)

❑ ❑   12 - Pel and the Touch of Pitch
            [by Mark Hebden] (1987)
❑ ❑   13 - Pel and the Picture of Innocence
            [by Mark Hebden] (1989)
❑ ❑   14 - Pel and the Party Spirit
            [by Mark Hebden] (1989)
❑ ❑   15 - Pel and the Missing Persons
            [by Mark Hebden] (1990)
❑ ❑   16 - Pel and the Promised Land
            [by Mark Hebden] (1991)
❑ ❑   17 - Pel and the Sepulchre
            [by Mark Hebden] (1992)
❑ ❑   18 - Pel Picks up the Pieces (1993)
❑ ❑   19 - Pel and the Perfect Partner (1995)
❑ ❑   20 - Pel is Provoked (1998)
❑ ❑   21 - Pel and the Precious Parcel (1997)
❑ ❑   . . . .
❑ ❑   . . . .

HENDERSON, Lauren

Sam Jones

❑ ❑   1 - Dead White Female (1995)
❑ ❑   2 - Too Many Blondes (1996)
❑ ❑   3 - Black Rubber Dress (1997)
❑ ❑   4 - Freeze My Margarita (1998)
❑ ❑   . . . .
❑ ❑   . . . .

HENDRICKSEN, Louise

Amy Prescott

❑ ❑   1 - With Deadly Intent (1993)
❑ ❑   2 - Grave Secrets (1994)
❑ ❑   3 - Lethal Legacy (1995)
❑ ❑   . . . .
❑ ❑   . . . .

HENRY, Sue

Jessie Arnold & Alex Jensen

❑ ❑   1 - Murder on the Iditarod Trail (1991)★★
❑ ❑   2 - Termination Dust (1995)

❑ ❑   3 - Sleeping Lady (1996)
❑ ❑   4 - Death Takes Passage (1997)
❑ ❑   5 - Deadfall (1998)
❑ ❑   . . . .
❑ ❑   . . . .

HERNDON, Nancy

Elena Jarvis

❑ ❑   1 - Acid Bath (1995)
❑ ❑   2 - Widows' Watch (1995)
❑ ❑   3 - Lethal Statues (1996)
❑ ❑   4 - Hunting Game (1996)
❑ ❑   5 - Time Bombs (1997)
❑ ❑   6 - C.O.P. Out (1998)
❑ ❑   . . . .
❑ ❑   . . . .

HERON, Echo

Adele Monsarrat

❑ ❑   1 - Pulse (1998)
❑ ❑   2 - Panic (1998)
❑ ❑   3 - Paradox (1999)
❑ ❑   . . . .
❑ ❑   . . . .

HESS, Joan

Arly Hanks

❑ ❑   1 - Malice in Maggody (1987)
❑ ❑   2 - Mischief in Maggody (1988)☆☆
❑ ❑   3 - Much Ado in Maggody (1989)
❑ ❑   4 - Mortal Remains in Maggody (1991)
❑ ❑   5 - Madness in Maggody (1991)
❑ ❑   6 - Maggody in Manhattan (1992)
❑ ❑   7 - O Little Town of Maggody (1993)☆☆
❑ ❑   8 - Martians in Maggody (1994)
❑ ❑   9 - Miracles in Maggody (1995)☆
❑ ❑   10 - The Maggody Militia (1997)
❑ ❑   11 - Misery in Maggody (1998)
❑ ❑   . . . .
❑ ❑   . . . .

Claire Malloy

- ❏ ❏   1 - Strangled Prose (1986)☆
- ❏ ❏   2 - The Murder at the Murder at the Mimosa Inn (1986)
- ❏ ❏   3 - Dear Miss Demeanor (1987)
- ❏ ❏   4 - A Really Cute Corpse (1988)
- ❏ ❏   5 - A Diet to Die For (1989)★
- ❏ ❏   6 - Roll Over and Play Dead (1991)
- ❏ ❏   7 - Death by the Light of the Moon (1992)
- ❏ ❏   8 - Poisoned Pins (1993)
- ❏ ❏   9 - Tickled to Death (1994)
- ❏ ❏ 10 - Busy Bodies (1995)
- ❏ ❏ 11 - Closely Akin to Murder (1996)
- ❏ ❏ 12 - A Holly, Jolly Murder (1997)
- ❏ ❏   . . . .
- ❏ ❏   . . . .

HIGHSMITH, Domini

Father Simeon & Elvira

- ❏ ❏   1 - Keeper at the Shrine (1994)
- ❏ ❏   2 - Guardian at the Gate (1995)
- ❏ ❏   3 - Master of the Keys (1996)
- ❏ ❏   . . . .
- ❏ ❏   . . . .

HIGHTOWER, Lynn S.

David Silver & String

- ❏ ❏   1 - Alien Blues (1992)
- ❏ ❏   2 - Alien Eyes (1993)
- ❏ ❏   3 - Alien Heat (1994)
- ❏ ❏   4 - Alien Rites (1995)
- ❏ ❏   . . . .
- ❏ ❏   . . . .

Lena Padget

- ❏ ❏   1 - Satan's Lambs (1993)★
- ❏ ❏   . . . .
- ❏ ❏   . . . .

Sonora Blair

❏ ❏   1 - Flashpoint (1995)
❏ ❏   2 - Eyeshot (1995)
❏ ❏   3 - No Good Deed (1998)
❏ ❏   . . . .
❏ ❏   . . . .

HOFF, B. J.

David & Jennifer Kaine

❏ ❏   1 - Mists of Danger (1986)
❏ ❏   2 - Storm at Daybreak (1986)
❏ ❏   3 - The Domino Image (1987)
❏ ❏   4 - The Tangled Web (1988)
❏ ❏   5 - Vow of Silence (1988)
❏ ❏   6 - Dark River Legacy (1990)
❏ ❏   . . . .
❏ ❏   . . . .

HOLBROOK, Teri

Gale Grayson

❏ ❏   1 - A Far and Deadly Cry (1995)☆☆☆
❏ ❏   2 - The Grass Widow (1996)☆☆☆☆
❏ ❏   3 - Sad Water (1999)
❏ ❏   . . . .
❏ ❏   . . . .

HOLLAND, Isabelle

Claire Aldington

❏ ❏   1 - The Lost Madonna (1983)
❏ ❏   2 - A Death at St. Anselm's (1984)
❏ ❏   3 - Flight of the Archangel (1985)
❏ ❏   4 - A Lover Scorned (1986)
❏ ❏   5 - A Fatal Advent (1989)
❏ ❏   6 - The Long Search (1990)
❏ ❏   . . . .
❏ ❏   . . . .

HOLMS, Joyce

Tam Buchanan & Fizz

❏ ❏   1 - Payment Deferred (1996)
❏ ❏   2 - Foreign Body (1997)
❏ ❏   3 - Bad Vibes (1998)
❏ ❏   . . . .
❏ ❏   . . . .

HOLT, Hazel

Sheila Malory

❏ ❏   1 - Mrs. Malory Investigates (1989)
❏ ❏   -Brit.-Gone Away
❏ ❏   2 - The Cruellest Month (1991)
❏ ❏   3 - The Shortest Journey (1992)
❏ ❏   4 - Mrs. Malory and the Festival Murders (1993)
❏ ❏   -Brit.-Uncertain Death
❏ ❏   5 - Mrs. Malory: Detective in Residence (1994)
❏ ❏   -Brit.-Murder on Campus
❏ ❏   6 - Mrs. Malory Wonders Why (1995)
❏ ❏   -Brit.-Superfluous Death
❏ ❏   7 - Mrs. Malory: Death of a Dean (1996)
❏ ❏   8 - Dead and Buried (1998)
❏ ❏   . . . .
❏ ❏   . . . .

HOLTZER, Susan

Anneke Haagen

❏ ❏   1 - Something To Kill For (1994)★
❏ ❏   2 - Curly Smoke (1995)
❏ ❏   3 - Bleeding Maize and Blue (1996)
❏ ❏   4 - Black Diamond (1997)
❏ ❏   5 - The Silly Season (1999)
❏ ❏   . . . .
❏ ❏   . . . .

HOOPER, Kay

Hagen
- ❏ ❏ 1 - In Serena's Web (1987)
- ❏ ❏ 2 - Raven on the Wing (1987)
- ❏ ❏ 3 - Rafferty's Wife (1987)
- ❏ ❏ 4 - Zach's Law (1987)
- ❏ ❏ 5 - The Fall of Lucas Kendrick (1988)
- ❏ ❏ 6 - Unmasking Kelsey (1988)
- ❏ ❏ 7 - Outlaw Derek (1988)
- ❏ ❏ 8 - Shades of Gray (1988)
- ❏ ❏ 9 - Captain's Paradise (1988)
- ❏ ❏ 10 - It Takes a Thief (1989)
- ❏ ❏ 11 - Aces High (1989)
- ❏ ❏ . . . .
- ❏ ❏ . . . .

Lane Montana & Trey Fortier
- ❏ ❏ 1 - Crime of Passion (1991)
- ❏ ❏ 2 - House of Cards (1991)☆
- ❏ ❏ . . . .
- ❏ ❏ . . . .

HORANSKY, Ruby [P]

Nikki Trakos
- ❏ ❏ 1 - Dead Ahead (1990)
- ❏ ❏ 2 - Dead Center (1994)
- ❏ ❏ . . . .
- ❏ ❏ . . . .

HORNSBY, Wendy

Kate Teague & Roger Tejeda
- ❏ ❏ 1 - No Harm (1987)
- ❏ ❏ 2 - Half a Mind (1990)
- ❏ ❏ . . . .
- ❏ ❏ . . . .

Maggie MacGowen

❏ ❏ 1 - Telling Lies (1992)
❏ ❏ 2 - Midnight Baby (1993)
❏ ❏ 3 - Bad Intent (1994)
❏ ❏ 4 - 77th Street Requiem (1995)
❏ ❏ 5 - A Hard Light (1997)
❏ ❏ . . . .
❏ ❏ . . . .

HOROWITZ, Renee B.

Ruthie Kantor Morris

❏ ❏ 1 - Rx for Murder (1997)
❏ ❏ 2 - Deadly Rx (1997)
❏ ❏ . . . .
❏ ❏ . . . .

HOWE, Melodie Johnson

Claire Conrad & Maggie Hill

❏ ❏ 1 - The Mother Shadow (1989)☆☆☆
❏ ❏ 2 - Beauty Dies (1994)
❏ ❏ . . . .
❏ ❏ . . . .

HOWELL, Lis

Kate Wilkinson

❏ ❏ 1 - After the Break (1995)
❏ ❏ 2 - The Director's Cut (1996)
❏ ❏ 3 - A Job To Die For (1997)
❏ ❏ . . . .
❏ ❏ . . . .

HUFF, Tanya

Vicki Nelson

❏ ❏ 1 - Blood Price (1992)
❏ ❏ 2 - Blood Trail (1992)
❏ ❏ 3 - Blood Lines (1993)
❏ ❏ 4 - Blood Pact (1993)
❏ ❏ . . . .
❏ ❏ . . . .

HYDE, Eleanor

Lydia Miller

❏ ❏   1 - In Murder We Trust (1995)
❏ ❏   2 - Animal Instincts (1996)
❏ ❏   . . . .
❏ ❏   . . . .

IAKOVOU, Takis and Judy

Nick & Julia Lambros

- ❏ ❏   1 - So Dear to Wicked Men (1996)
- ❏ ❏   2 - Go Close Against the Enemy (1998)
- ❏ ❏   . . . .
- ❏ ❏   . . . .

JACKSON, Hialeah [P]

Annabelle Hardy-Maratos & Dave the Monkeyman

❏ ❏ 1 - The Alligator's Farewell (1998)
❏ ❏ 2 - Farewell, Butterfly Sue (1999)
❏ ❏ . . . .
❏ ❏ . . . .

JACKSON, Marian J. A.

Abigail Patience Danforth

❏ ❏ 1 - The Punjat's Ruby (1990)
❏ ❏ 2 - The Arabian Pearl (1990)
❏ ❏ 3 - Cat's Eye (1991)
❏ ❏ 4 - Diamond Head (1992)
❏ ❏ 5 - The Sunken Treasure (1994)
❏ ❏ . . . .
❏ ❏ . . . .

JACOBS, Jonnie

Kali O'Brien

❏ ❏ 1 - Shadow of Doubt (1996)
❏ ❏ 2 - Evidence of Guilt (1997)
❏ ❏ 3 - Motion to Dismiss (1999)
❏ ❏ . . . .
❏ ❏ . . . .

Kate Austen

❏ ❏ 1 - Murder Among Neighbors (1994)
❏ ❏ 2 - Murder Among Friends (1995)
❏ ❏ 3 - Murder Among Us (1998)
❏ ❏ . . . .
❏ ❏ . . . .

JACOBS, Nancy Baker

Devon MacDonald

❏ ❏ 1 - The Turquoise Tattoo (1991)
❏ ❏ 2 - A Slash of Scarlet (1992)
❏ ❏ 3 - The Silver Scalpel (1993)
❏ ❏ . . . .
❏ ❏ . . . .

JAFFE, Jody

Natalie Gold

❏ ❏ 1 - Horse of a Different Killer (1995)☆☆
❏ ❏ 2 - Chestnut Mare, Beware (1996)
❏ ❏ 3 - In Colt Blood (1998)
❏ ❏ . . . .
❏ ❏ . . . .

JAKEMAN, Jane

Ambrose Malfine

❏ ❏ 1 - Let There Be Blood (1997)
❏ ❏ 2 - The Egyptian Coffin (1998)
❏ ❏ . . . .
❏ ❏ . . . .

JAMES, P. D.

Adam Dalgleish

❏ ❏ 1 - Cover Her Face (1962)
❏ ❏ 2 - A Mind to Murder (1963)
❏ ❏ 3 - Unnatural Causes (1967)
❏ ❏ 4 - Shroud for a Nightingale (1971)★☆
❏ ❏ 5 - The Black Tower (1975)★
❏ ❏ 6 - Death of an Expert Witness (1977)
❏ ❏ 7 - A Taste for Death (1986)★★
❏ ❏ 8 - Devices and Desires (1989)
❏ ❏ 9 - Original Sin (1994)
❏ ❏ 10 - A Certain Justice (1998)
❏ ❏ . . . .
❏ ❏ . . . .

Cordelia Gray

❏ ❏ 1 - An Unsuitable Job for a Woman (1972)☆
❏ ❏ 2 - The Skull Beneath the Skin (1982)
❏ ❏ . . . .
❏ ❏ . . . .

JANCE, J. A.

J. P. Beaumont

❑ ❑   1 - Until Proven Guilty (1985)
❑ ❑   2 - Injustice for All (1986)
❑ ❑   3 - Trial by Fury (1986)
❑ ❑   4 - Taking the Fifth (1987)
❑ ❑   5 - Improbable Cause (1988)
❑ ❑   6 - A More Perfect Union (1988)
❑ ❑   7 - Dismissed With Prejudice (1989)
❑ ❑   8 - Minor in Possession (1990)
❑ ❑   9 - Payment in Kind (1991)
❑ ❑ 10 - Without Due Process (1992)★
❑ ❑ 11 - Failure to Appear (1993)★
❑ ❑ 12 - Lying in Wait (1994)
❑ ❑ 13 - Name Withheld (1995)
❑ ❑ 14 - Breach of Duty (1999)
❑ ❑   . . . .
❑ ❑   . . . .

Joanna Brady

❑ ❑   1 - Desert Heat (1993)
❑ ❑   2 - Tombstone Courage (1994)
❑ ❑   3 - Shoot, Don't Shoot (1995)
❑ ❑   4 - Dead to Rights (1996)
❑ ❑   5 - Skeleton Canyon (1997)
❑ ❑   6 - Rattlesnake Crossing (1998)
❑ ❑   7 - Outlaw Mountain (1999)
❑ ❑   . . . .
❑ ❑   . . . .

JENNINGS, Maureen

William Murdoch

❑ ❑   1 - Except the Dying (1997)
❑ ❑   2 - Under the Dragon's Tail (1998)
❑ ❑   . . . .
❑ ❑   . . . .

JOHN, Cathie [P]
Kate Cavanaugh

❏ ❏   1 - Add One Dead Critic (1997)
❏ ❏   2 - Beat a Rotten Egg to the Punch (1998)
❏ ❏   3 - Carve a Witness to Shreds (1999)
❏ ❏   4 - Debone a Killer's Alibi (2000)
❏ ❏   . . . .
❏ ❏   . . . .

JOHN, Katherine
Trevor Joseph

❏ ❏   1 - Without Trace (1995)
❏ ❏   2 - Six Foot Under (1996)
❏ ❏   3 - Murder of a Dead Man (1997)
❏ ❏   4 - By Any Other Name (1998)
❏ ❏   . . . .
❏ ❏   . . . .

JOHNSON, Barbara
Colleen Fitzgerald

❏ ❏   1 - The Beach Affair (1995)
❏ ❏   2 - Bad Moon Rising (1998)
❏ ❏   . . . .
❏ ❏   . . . .

JOHNSON, Dolores
Mandy Dyer

❏ ❏   1 - Taken to the Cleaners (1997)
❏ ❏   2 - Hung Up to Die (1997)
❏ ❏   3 - A Dress To Die For (1998)
❏ ❏   . . . .
❏ ❏   . . . .

JOHNSTON, Jane
Louisa Evans

❏ ❏   1 - Pray for Ricky Foster (1985)
❏ ❏   2 - Paint Her Face Dead (1987)
❏ ❏   . . . .
❏ ❏   . . . .

JONES, D. J. H. [P]

Nancy Cook

❏ ❏   1 - Murder at the MLA (1993)
❏ ❏   2 - Murder in the New Age (1997)
❏ ❏   ....
❏ ❏   ....

JORDAN, Jennifer

Barry & Dee Vaughan

❏ ❏   1 - A Good Weekend for Murder (1987)
❏ ❏   2 - Murder Under the Mistletoe (1988)
❏ ❏   3 - Book Early for Murder (1990)
❏ ❏   ....
❏ ❏   ....

JORDAN, Jennifer

Kristin Ashe

❏ ❏   1 - A Safe Place to Sleep (1992)
❏ ❏   2 - Existing Solutions (1993)
❏ ❏   ....
❏ ❏   ....

JORGENSEN, Christine T.

Stella the Stargazer

❏ ❏   1 - A Love to Die For (1994)
❏ ❏   2 - You Bet Your Life (1995)
❏ ❏   3 - Curl Up and Die (1996)
❏ ❏   4 - Death of a Dustbunny (1998)
❏ ❏   ....
❏ ❏   ....

JOSEPH, Alison

Agnes Bourdillon

❏ ❏   1 - Sacred Hearts (1994)
❏ ❏   2 - The Hour of Our Death (1995)
❏ ❏   3 - The Quick and the Dead (1996)
❏ ❏   4 - A Dark and Sinful Death (1997)
❏ ❏   ....
❏ ❏   ....

KAEWERT, Julie Wallin

Alex Plumtree

❑ ❑ 1 - Unsolicited (1994)
❑ ❑ 2 - Unbound (1997)
❑ ❑ . . . .
❑ ❑ . . . .

KAHN, Sharon

Ruby Rothman

❑ ❑ 1 - Fax Me a Bagel (1998)
❑ ❑ 2 - Never Nosh a Matzo Ball (1999)
❑ ❑ . . . .
❑ ❑ . . . .

KALLEN, Lucille

Maggie Rome & C.B. Greenfield

❑ ❑ 1 - Introducing C.B. Greenfield (1979)
❑ ❑ 2 - The Tanglewood Murder (1980)
❑ ❑ 3 - No Lady in the House (1982)
❑ ❑ 4 - The Piano Bird (1984)
❑ ❑ 5 - A Little Madness (1986)
❑ ❑ . . . .
❑ ❑ . . . .

KELLERMAN, Faye

Peter Decker & Rina Lazarus

❑ ❑   1 - The Ritual Bath (1986)★
❑ ❑   2 - Sacred and Profane (1987)
❑ ❑   3 - Milk and Honey (1990)
❑ ❑   4 - Day of Atonement (1992)
❑ ❑   5 - False Prophet (1992)
❑ ❑   6 - Grievous Sin (1993)
❑ ❑   7 - Sanctuary (1994)
❑ ❑   8 - Justice (1995)
❑ ❑   9 - Prayers for the Dead (1996)
❑ ❑ 10 - A Serpent's Tooth (1997)
❑ ❑ . . . .
❑ ❑ . . . .

KELLOGG, Marne Davis

Lilly Bennett

❑ ❑   1 - Bad Manners (1995)
❑ ❑   2 - Curtsey (1996)
❑ ❑   3 - Tramp (1997)
❑ ❑   4 - Nothing But Gossip (1998)
❑ ❑   5 - The Birthday Party (2000)
❑ ❑   . . . .
❑ ❑   . . . .

KELLY, Mary

Brett Nightingale

❑ ❑   1 - A Cold Coming (1956)
❑ ❑   2 - Dead Man's Riddle (1957)
❑ ❑   3 - The Christmas Egg (1958)
❑ ❑   . . . .
❑ ❑   . . . .

Hedley Nicholson

❑ ❑   1 - The Spoilt Kill (1961)★
❑ ❑   2 - Due to a Death (1962)
❑ ❑   - U.S.-The Dead of Summer
❑ ❑   . . . .
❑ ❑   . . . .

KELLY, Mary Ann

Claire Breslinsky

❑ ❑   1 - Parklane South, Queens (1990)
❑ ❑   2 - Foxglove (1992)
❑ ❑   3 - Keeper of the Mill (1995)
❑ ❑   . . . .
❑ ❑   . . . .

KELLY, Nora

Gillian Adams

❑ ❑   1 - In the Shadow of King's (1984)
❑ ❑   2 - My Sister's Keeper (1992)
❑ ❑   3 - Bad Chemistry (1993)
❑ ❑   4 - Old Wounds (1998)
❑ ❑   . . . .
❑ ❑   . . . .

KELLY, Susan

Liz Connors

- ❑ ❑ 1 - The Gemini Man (1985)☆
- ❑ ❑ 2 - The Summertime Soldiers (1986)
- ❑ ❑ 3 - Trail of the Dragon (1988)
- ❑ ❑ 4 - Until Proven Innocent (1990)
- ❑ ❑ 5 - And Soon I'll Come to Kill You (1991)
- ❑ ❑ 6 - Out of the Darkness (1992)
- ❑ ❑ . . . .
- ❑ ❑ . . . .

KELLY, Susan B.

Alison Hope & Nick Trevellyan

- ❑ ❑ 1 - Hope Against Hope (1990)
- ❑ ❑ 2 - Time of Hope (1990)
- ❑ ❑ 3 - Hope Will Answer (1993)
- ❑ ❑ 4 - Kid's Stuff (1994)
- ❑ ❑ 5 - Death is Sweet (1996)
- ❑ ❑ . . . .
- ❑ ❑ . . . .

KELNER, Toni L. P.

Laura Fleming

- ❑ ❑ 1 - Down Home Murder (1993)
- ❑ ❑ 2 - Dead Ringer (1994)
- ❑ ❑ 3 - Trouble Looking for a Place to Happen (1995)
- ❑ ❑ 4 - Country Comes to Town (1996)
- ❑ ❑ 5 - Tight as a Tick (1998)
- ❑ ❑ 6 - Death of a Damn Yankee (1999)
- ❑ ❑ . . . .
- ❑ ❑ . . . .

KENNETT, Shirley

P J Gray

- ❑ ❑ 1 - Gray Matter (1996)
- ❑ ❑ 2 - Fire Cracker (1997)
- ❑ ❑ 3 - Chameleon (1998)
- ❑ ❑ 4 - Wild Justice (1999)
- ❑ ❑ . . . .
- ❑ ❑ . . . .

KENNEY, Susan

Roz Howard & Alan Stewart

❑ ❑   1 - Garden of Malice (1983)
❑ ❑   2 - Graves of Academe (1985)
❑ ❑   3 - One Fell Sloop (1990)
❑ ❑   . . . .
❑ ❑   . . . .

KERSHAW, Valerie

Mitch Mitchell

❑ ❑   1 - Murder Is Too Expensive (1993)
❑ ❑   2 - Funny Money (1994)
❑ ❑   3 - Late Knights (1995)
❑ ❑   . . . .
❑ ❑   . . . .

KIECOLT-GLASER, Janice

Haley McAlister

❑ ❑   1 - Detecting Lies (1997)
❑ ❑   2 - Unconscious Truths (1998)
❑ ❑   . . . .
❑ ❑   . . . .

KIJEWSKI, Karen

Kat Colorado

❑ ❑   1 - Katwalk (1988)★★★
❑ ❑   2 - Katapult (1990)
❑ ❑   3 - Kat's Cradle (1991)
❑ ❑   4 - Copy Kat (1992)
❑ ❑   5 - Wild Kat (1994)
❑ ❑   6 - Alley Cat Blues (1995)
❑ ❑   7 - Honky Tonk Kat (1996)
❑ ❑   8 - Kat Scratch Fever (1997)
❑ ❑   9 - Stray Kat Waltz (1998)
❑ ❑   . . . .
❑ ❑   . . . .

KING, Laurie R.

Kate Martinelli & Alonzo Hawkin

❏ ❏   1 - A Grave Talent (1993)★☆☆
❏ ❏   2 - To Play the Fool (1995)
❏ ❏   3 - With Child (1996)
❏ ❏   . . . .
❏ ❏   . . . .

Mary Russell

❏ ❏   1 - The Beekeeper's Apprentice (1994)☆
❏ ❏   2 - A Monstrous Regiment of Women (1995)★
❏ ❏   3 - A Letter of Mary (1996)
❏ ❏   4 - The Moor (1998)
❏ ❏   . . . .
❏ ❏   . . . .

KINGSBURY, Kate [P]

Cecily Sinclair

❏ ❏   1 - Room With a Clue (1993)
❏ ❏   2 - Do Not Disturb (1994)
❏ ❏   3 - Service for Two (1994)
❏ ❏   4 - Eat, Drink, and Be Buried (1994)
❏ ❏   5 - Check-out Time (1995)
❏ ❏   6 - Grounds for Murder (1995)
❏ ❏   7 - Pay the Piper (1996)
❏ ❏   8 - Chivalry Is Dead (1996)
❏ ❏   9 - Ring for Tomb Service (1997)
❏ ❏   10 - Death With Reservations (1998)
❏ ❏   11 - Dying Room Only (1998)
❏ ❏   . . . .
❏ ❏   . . . .

KITTREDGE, Mary

Charlotte Kent

❏ ❏   1 - Murder in Mendocino (1987)
❏ ❏   2 - Dead and Gone (1989)
❏ ❏   3 - Poison Pen (1990)
❏ ❏   . . . .
❏ ❏   . . . .

Edwina Crusoe

❑ ❑   1 - Fatal Diagnosis (1990)
❑ ❑   2 - Rigor Mortis (1991)
❑ ❑   3 - Cadaver (1992)
❑ ❑   4 - Walking Dead Man (1992)
❑ ❑   5 - Desperate Remedy (1993)
❑ ❑   6 - Kill or Cure (1995)
❑ ❑   . . . .
❑ ❑   . . . .

KNIGHT, Alanna

Jeremy Faro

❑ ❑   1 - Enter Second Murderer (1988)
❑ ❑   2 - Blood Line (1989)
❑ ❑   3 - Deadly Beloved (1989)
❑ ❑   4 - Killing Cousins (1990)
❑ ❑   5 - A Quiet Death (1991)
❑ ❑   6 - To Kill a Queen (1992)
❑ ❑   7 - The Evil That Men Do (1993)
❑ ❑   8 - The Missing Duchess (1994)
❑ ❑   9 - The Bull Slayers (1995)
❑ ❑ 10 - Murder by Appointment (1996)
❑ ❑ 11 - The Coffin Lane Murders (1998)
❑ ❑   . . . .
❑ ❑   . . . .

KNIGHT, KATHRYN LASKY

Calista Jacobs

❑ ❑   1 - Trace Elements (1986)
❑ ❑   2 - Mortal Words (1990)
❑ ❑   3 - Mumbo Jumbo (1991)
❑ ❑   4 - Dark Swain (1994)
❑ ❑   . . . .
❑ ❑   . . . .

KNIGHT, Phyllis
Lil Ritchie
❏ ❏   1 - Switching the Odds (1992)☆
❏ ❏   2 - Shattered Rhythms (1994)
❏ ❏   . . . .
❏ ❏   . . . .

KRAFT, Gabrielle
Jerry Zalman
❏ ❏   1 - Bullshot (1987)☆
❏ ❏   2 - Screwdriver (1988)
❏ ❏   3 - Let's Rob Roy (1989)
❏ ❏   4 - Bloody Mary (1990)
❏ ❏   . . . .
❏ ❏   . . . .

KRICH, Rochelle Majer
Debra Laslow
❏ ❏   1 - Speak No Evil (1996)
❏ ❏   . . . .
❏ ❏   . . . .

Jessie Drake
❏ ❏   1 - Fair Game (1993)☆
❏ ❏   2 - Angel of Death (1994)☆
❏ ❏   3 - Blood Money (1999)
❏ ❏   . . . .
❏ ❏   . . . .

KRUGER, Mary
Brooke Cassidy & Matt Devlin
❏ ❏   1 - Death on the Cliff Walk (1994)
❏ ❏   2 - No Honeymoon for Death (1995)
❏ ❏   3 - Masterpiece of Murder (1996)
❏ ❏   . . . .
❏ ❏   . . . .

LACEY, Sarah

Leah Hunter

❏ ❏   1 - File Under: Deceased (1992)
❏ ❏   2 - File Under: Missing (1993)
❏ ❏   3 - File Under: Arson (1994)
❏ ❏   4 - File Under: Jeopardy (1995)
❏ ❏   . . . .
❏ ❏   . . . .

LACHNIT, Carroll

Hannah Barlow

❏ ❏   1 - Murder in Brief (1995)
❏ ❏   2 - A Blessed Death (1996)
❏ ❏   3 - Akin to Death (1998)
❏ ❏   . . . .
❏ ❏   . . . .

LACKEY, Mercedes

Diana Tregarde

❏ ❏   1 - Burning Water (1989)
❏ ❏   2 - Children of the Night (1990)
❏ ❏   3 - Jinx High (1991)
❏ ❏   . . . .
❏ ❏   . . . .

LAKE, Deryn [P]

John Rawlings & the Blind Beak

❏ ❏   1 - Death in the Dark Walk (1994)
❏ ❏   2 - Death at the Beggar's Opera (1995)
❏ ❏   3 - Death at the Devil's Tavern (1996)
❏ ❏   4 - Death on the Romney Marsh (1998)
❏ ❏   . . . .
❏ ❏   . . . .

LAMB, J. Dayne

Teal Stewart

- ❏ ❏   1 - Questionable Behavior (1993)
- ❏ ❏   2 - A Question of Preference (1994)
- ❏ ❏   3 - Unquestioned Loyalty (1995)
- ❏ ❏   . . . .
- ❏ ❏   . . . .

LAMBERT, Mercedes

Whitney Logan

- ❏ ❏   1 - Dogtown (1991)
- ❏ ❏   2 - Soultown (1996)
- ❏ ❏   . . . .
- ❏ ❏   . . . .

LANDRETH, Marsha

Samantha Turner

- ❏ ❏   1 - The Holiday Murders (1992)
- ❏ ❏   2 - A Clinic for Murder (1993)
- ❏ ❏   3 - Vial Murders (1995)
- ❏ ❏   . . . .
- ❏ ❏   . . . .

LANGTON, Jane

Homer Kelly

- ❏ ❏   1 - The Transcendental Murder (1964)
- ❏ ❏   - APA-The Minuteman Murder (1976)
- ❏ ❏   2 - Dark Nantucket Noon (1975)
- ❏ ❏   3 - The Memorial Hall Murder (1978)
- ❏ ❏   4 - Natural Enemy (1982)
- ❏ ❏   5 - Emily Dickinson Is Dead (1984)★☆
- ❏ ❏   6 - Good and Dead (1986)
- ❏ ❏   7 - Murder at the Gardner (1988)
- ❏ ❏   8 - The Dante Game (1991)
- ❏ ❏   9 - God in Concord (1992)
- ❏ ❏   10 - Divine Inspiration (1993)

❏ ❏ 11 - The Shortest Day (1995)
❏ ❏ 12 - Dead as a Dodo (1996)
❏ ❏ 13 - The Face on the Wall (1998)
❏ ❏ . . . .
❏ ❏ . . . .

LANIER, Virginia

Jo Beth Sidden

❏ ❏ 1 - Death in Bloodhound Red (1995)★☆☆
❏ ❏ 2 - The House on Bloodhound Lane (1996)
❏ ❏ 3 - A Brace of Bloodhounds (1997)
❏ ❏ 4 - Blind Bloodhound Justice (1998)
❏ ❏ . . . .
❏ ❏ . . . .

LaPIERRE, Janet

Vince Gutierrez & Meg Halloran

❏ ❏ 1 - Unquiet Grave (1987)☆
❏ ❏ 2 - Children's Games (1989)
❏ ❏ 3 - Cruel Mother (1990)
❏ ❏ 4 - Grandmother's House (1991)
❏ ❏ 5 - Old Enemies (1993)☆
❏ ❏ . . . .
❏ ❏ . . . .

LaPLANTE, Lynda

Dolly Rawlins

❏ ❏ 1 - The Widows (1983)
❏ ❏ 2 - The Widows II (1985)
❏ ❏ 3 - She's Out (1995)
❏ ❏ 4 - Trial and Retribution (1997)
❏ ❏ 5 - Trial and Retribution II (1998)
❏ ❏ . . . .
❏ ❏ . . . .

Jane Tennison

❏ ❏ 1 - Prime Suspect (1993)
❏ ❏ 2 - Prime Suspect 2 (1993)
❏ ❏ 3 - Prime Suspect 3 (1994)
❏ ❏ . . . .
❏ ❏ . . . .

Lorraine Page

❏ ❏   1 - Cold Shoulder (1994)
❏ ❏   2 - Cold Blood (1996)
❏ ❏   3 - Cold Heart (1998)
❏ ❏   . . . .
❏ ❏   . . . .

LATHEN, Emma [P]

John Putnam Thatcher

❏ ❏   1 - Banking on Death (1961)
❏ ❏   2 - A Place for Murder (1963)
❏ ❏   3 - Accounting for Murder (1964)★
❏ ❏   4 - Murder Makes the Wheels Go 'Round (1966)
❏ ❏   5 - Death Shall Overcome (1966)
❏ ❏   6 - Murder Against the Grain (1967)★
❏ ❏   7 - A Stitch in Time (1968)
❏ ❏   8 - Come to Dust (1968)
❏ ❏   9 - When in Greece (1969)☆
❏ ❏ 10 - Murder To Go (1969)
❏ ❏ 11 - Pick up Sticks (1970)
❏ ❏ 12 - Ashes to Ashes (1971)
❏ ❏ 13 - The Longer the Thread (1971)
❏ ❏ 14 - Murder Without Icing (1972)
❏ ❏ 15 - Sweet and Low (1974)
❏ ❏ 16 - By Hook or by Crook (1975)
❏ ❏ 17 - Double, Double, Oil and Trouble (1978)
❏ ❏ 18 - Going for the Gold (1981)
❏ ❏ 19 - Green Grow the Dollars (1982)★
❏ ❏ 20 - Something in the Air (1988)
❏ ❏ 21 - East Is East (1991)
❏ ❏ 22 - Right on the Money (1993)
❏ ❏ 23 - Brewing Up a Storm (1996)
❏ ❏ 24 - A Shark Out of Water (1997)
❏ ❏   . . . .
❏ ❏   . . . .

LAURENCE, Janet

Canaletto & Fanny

❏ ❏   1 - Canaletto and the Case of the Westminster Bridge (1998)

❏ ❏   2 - The Case of the Privvy Garden (1998)

❏ ❏   . . . .

❏ ❏   . . . .

Darina Lisle

❏ ❏   1 - A Deepe Coffyn (1989)

❏ ❏   2 - A Tasty Way to Die (1990)

❏ ❏   3 - Hotel Morgue (1991)

❏ ❏   4 - Recipe for Death (1992)

❏ ❏   5 - Death and the Epicure (1993)

❏ ❏   6 - Death at the Table (1994)

❏ ❏   7 - Death a la Provencale (1995)

❏ ❏   8 - Diet for Death (1996)

❏ ❏   9 - Death at the Table (1997)

❏ ❏   . . . .

❏ ❏   . . . .

LAW, Janice

Anna Peters

❏ ❏   1 - The Big Pay-off (1976)☆

❏ ❏   2 - Gemini Trip (1977)

❏ ❏   3 - Under Orion (1978)

❏ ❏   4 - The Shadow of the Palms (1980)

❏ ❏   5 - Death Under Par (1981)

❏ ❏   6 - Time Lapse (1992)

❏ ❏   7 - A Safe Place to Die (1993)

❏ ❏   8 - Backfire (1994)

❏ ❏   9 - Cross-Check (1997)

❏ ❏   . . . .

❏ ❏   . . . .

LAWRENCE, Hilda

Mark East, Bessie Petty & Beulah Pond

❑ ❑   1 - Blood Upon the Snow (1944)
❑ ❑   2 - A Time to Die (1944)
❑ ❑   3 - Death of a Doll (1947)
❑ ❑   . . . .
❑ ❑   . . . .

LAWRENCE, Margaret [P]

Hannah Trevor

❑ ❑   1 - Hearts and Bones (1996)☆☆
❑ ❑   2 - Blood Red Roses (1997)
❑ ❑   3 - The Burning Bride (1998)
❑ ❑   . . . .
❑ ❑   . . . .

LAWRENCE, Martha

Elizabeth Chase

❑ ❑   1 - Murder in Scorpio (1995)☆☆☆
❑ ❑   2 - The Cold Heart of Capricorn (1997)
❑ ❑   3 - Aquarius Descending (1999)
❑ ❑   . . . .
❑ ❑   . . . .

LEE, Barbara

Eve Elliott

❑ ❑   1 - Death in Still Waters (1995)★
❑ ❑   2 - Final Closing (1997)
❑ ❑   3 - Dead Man's Fingers (1999)
❑ ❑   . . . .
❑ ❑   . . . .

LEE, Marie

Marguerite Smith

❑ ❑   1 - The Curious Cape Cod Skull (1995)
❑ ❑   2 - The Fatal Cape Cod Funeral (1996)
❑ ❑   3 - The Mysterious Cape Cod Manuscript (1997)
❑ ❑   . . . .
❑ ❑   . . . .

LEE, Wendi

Angela Matelli

- ❏ ❏   1 - The Good Daughter (1994)
- ❏ ❏   2 - Missing Eden (1996)
- ❏ ❏   3 - Deadbeat (1998)
- ❏ ❏   . . . .
- ❏ ❏   . . . .

Jefferson Birch

- ❏ ❏   1 - Rogue's Gold [as W.W. Lee] (1989)
- ❏ ❏   2 - Rustler's Venom [as W.W. Lee] (1990)
- ❏ ❏   3 - Rancher's Blood [as W.W. Lee] (1991)
- ❏ ❏   4 - Robber's Trail [as W.W. Lee] (1992)
- ❏ ❏   5 - Outlaw's Fortune [as W.W. Lee] (1993)
- ❏ ❏   6 - Cannon's Revenge [as W.W. Lee] (1995)
- ❏ ❏   . . . .
- ❏ ❏   . . . .

LEMARCHAND, Elizabeth

Tom Pollard & Gregory Toye

- ❏ ❏   1 - Death of an Old Girl (1967)
- ❏ ❏   2 - The Affacombe Affair (1968)
- ❏ ❏   3 - Alibi for a Corpse (1969)
- ❏ ❏   4 - Death on Doomsday (1971)
- ❏ ❏   5 - Cyanide With Compliments (1972)
- ❏ ❏   6 - Let or Hindrance (1973)
- ❏ ❏   - U.S.-No Vacation from Murder
- ❏ ❏   7 - Buried in the Past (1974)
- ❏ ❏   8 - Step in the Dark (1976)
- ❏ ❏   9 - Unhappy Returns (1977)
- ❏ ❏ 10 - Suddenly While Gardening (1978)
- ❏ ❏ 11 - Change for the Worse (1980)
- ❏ ❏ 12 - Nothing To Do With the Case (1981)
- ❏ ❏ 13 - Troubled Waters (1982)
- ❏ ❏ 14 - The Wheel Turns (1983)
- ❏ ❏ 15 - Light through the Glass (1984)
- ❏ ❏ 16 - Who Goes Home? (1986)
- ❏ ❏ 17 - The Glade Manor Murder (1988)
- ❏ ❏   . . . .
- ❏ ❏   . . . .

LEON, Donna
Guido Brunetti
- ❏ ❏ 1 - Death at la Fenice (1992)
- ❏ ❏ 2 - Death in a Strange Country (1993)
- ❏ ❏ 3 - Dressed for Death (1994)
- ❏ ❏   - Brit.-The Anonymous Venetian
- ❏ ❏ 4 - Death and Judgment (1995)
- ❏ ❏   - Brit.-A Venetian Reckoning
- ❏ ❏ 5 - Acqua Alta (1996)
- ❏ ❏   - U.S.-Death in High Water
- ❏ ❏ 6 - The Death of Faith (1997)
- ❏ ❏ 7 - A Noble Radiance (1998)
- ❏ ❏ 8 - Fatal Remedies (1999)
- ❏ ❏ . . . .
- ❏ ❏ . . . .

LEWIS, Sherry
Fred Vickery
- ❏ ❏ 1 - No Place for Secrets (1995)
- ❏ ❏ 2 - No Place Like Home (1996)
- ❏ ❏ 3 - No Place for Death (1996)
- ❏ ❏ 4 - No Place for Tears (1997)
- ❏ ❏ 5 - No Place for Sin (1997)
- ❏ ❏ . . . .
- ❏ ❏ . . . .

LIN-CHANDLER, Irene
Holly-Jean Ho
- ❏ ❏ 1 - The Healing of Holly-Jean (1995)
- ❏ ❏ 2 - Grievous Angel (1996)
- ❏ ❏ 3 - Soul Exile (1997)
- ❏ ❏ . . . .
- ❏ ❏ . . . .

LINSCOTT, Gillian
Birdie Linnet
- ❏ ❏ 1 - A Healthy Body (1984)
- ❏ ❏ 2 - Murder Makes Tracks (1985)
- ❏ ❏ 3 - A Whiff of Sulphur (1987)
- ❏ ❏ . . . .
- ❏ ❏ . . . .

Nell Bray

❏ ❏ 1 - Sister Beneath the Sheet (1991)
❏ ❏ 2 - Hanging on the Wire (1992)
❏ ❏ 3 - Stage Fright (1993)
❏ ❏ 4 - Widow's Peak (1994)
❏ ❏   - U.S.-An Easy Day for a Lady
❏ ❏ 5 - Crown Witness (1995)
❏ ❏ 6 - Dead Man's Sweetheart (1996)
❏ ❏   - U.S.-Dead Man's Music
❏ ❏ 7 - Dance on Blood (1998)
❏ ❏ . . . .
❏ ❏ . . . .

LIPPMAN, Laura

Tess Monaghan

❏ ❏ 1 - Baltimore Blues (1997)☆
❏ ❏ 2 - Charm City (1997)★☆
❏ ❏ 3 - Butchers Hill (1998)
❏ ❏ 4 - Gone to Texas (1999)
❏ ❏ . . . .
❏ ❏ . . . .

LIVESAY, Ann

Barry Ross

❏ ❏ 1 - The Isis Command (1998)
❏ ❏ 2 - Death in the Amazon (1998)
❏ ❏ 3 - The Madman of Mt. Everest (1999)
❏ ❏ 4 - The Chala Project [Grand Canyon] (1999)
❏ ❏ 5 - The Dinkum Deaths [Great Barrier Reef] (2000)
❏ ❏ . . . .
❏ ❏ . . . .

LOGAN, Margaret

Olivia Chapman

❏ ❏ 1 - Deathampton Summer (1988)
❏ ❏ 2 - The End of an Altruist (1994)
❏ ❏ 3 - Never Let a Stranger in Your House (1995)
❏ ❏ . . . .
❏ ❏ . . . .

LORDON, Randye

Sydney Sloane

❏ ❏   1 - Brotherly Love (1993)☆
❏ ❏   2 - Sister's Keeper (1994)
❏ ❏   3 - Father Forgive Me (1997)☆
❏ ❏   4 - Mother May I (1998)
❏ ❏   5 - Say Uncle (1998)
❏ ❏   . . . .
❏ ❏   . . . .

LORENS, M. K.

William Marlowe Sherman

❏ ❏   1 - Sweet Narcissus (1990)
❏ ❏   2 - Ropedancer's Fall (1990)
❏ ❏   3 - Deception Island (1991)
❏ ❏   4 - Dreamland (1992)
❏ ❏   5 - Sorrowheart (1993)
❏ ❏   . . . .
❏ ❏   . . . .

LOVETT, Sarah

Sylvia Strange

❏ ❏   1 - Dangerous Attachments (1995)
❏ ❏   2 - Acquired Motives (1996)
❏ ❏   3 - A Desperate Silence (1998)
❏ ❏   . . . .
❏ ❏   . . . .

LUCKE, Margaret

Jessica Randolph

❏ ❏   1 - A Relative Stranger (1991)☆
❏ ❏   2 - Bridge to Nowhere (1996)
❏ ❏   . . . .
❏ ❏   . . . .

LYNDS, Gayle
Sarah Walker & Liz Sansborough
❑ ❑ 1 - Masquerade (1996)
❑ ❑ 2 - "M" (2000)
❑ ❑ . . . .
❑ ❑ . . . .

LYONS, Nan & Ivan
Natasha O'Brien & Millie Ogden
❑ ❑ 1 - Someone Is Killing the Great Chefs of Europe (1976)
❑ ❑ 2 - Someone Is Killing the Great Chefs of America (1993)
❑ ❑ . . . .
❑ ❑ . . . .

MacDONALD, Marianne

Dido Hoare

- ❑ ❑ 1 - Death's Autograph (1997)
- ❑ ❑ 2 - Ghost Walk (1998)
- ❑ ❑ . . . .
- ❑ ❑ . . . .

MacDOUGAL, Bonnie

Jackson, Rieders

- ❑ ❑ 1 - Breach of Trust (1996)
- ❑ ❑ 2 - Angle of Impact (1998)
- ❑ ❑ 3 - Out of Order (1999)
- ❑ ❑ . . . .
- ❑ ❑ . . . .

MacGREGOR, T. J.

Quin St. James & Mike McCleary

- ❑ ❑ 1 - Dark Fields (1986)☆
- ❑ ❑ 2 - Kill Flash (1987)
- ❑ ❑ 3 - Death Sweet (1988)
- ❑ ❑ 4 - On Ice (1989)
- ❑ ❑ 5 - Kin Dread (1990)
- ❑ ❑ 6 - Death Flats (1991)
- ❑ ❑ 7 - Spree (1992)
- ❑ ❑ 8 - Storm Surge (1993)
- ❑ ❑ 9 - Blue Pearl (1994)
- ❑ ❑ 10 - Mistress of the Bones (1995)
- ❑ ❑ . . . .
- ❑ ❑ . . . .

MacKAY, Amanda

Hannah Land

- ❑ ❑ 1 - Murder Is Academic (1976)
- ❑ ❑ 2 - Death on the Eno (1981)
- ❑ ❑ . . . .
- ❑ ❑ . . . .

MacLEOD, Charlotte

Peter Shandy & Helen Marsh Shandy

❏ ❏   1 - Rest You Merry (1978)
❏ ❏   2 - The Luck Runs Out (1979)
❏ ❏   3 - Wrack and Rune (1982)
❏ ❏   4 - Something the Cat Dragged In (1983)
❏ ❏   5 - The Curse of the Giant Hogweed (1985)
❏ ❏   6 - The Corpse in Oozak's Pond (1986)★☆
❏ ❏   7 - Vane Pursuit (1989)
❏ ❏   8 - An Owl Too Many (1991)☆
❏ ❏   9 - Something in the Water (1994)
❏ ❏ 10 - Exit the Milkman (1996)
❏ ❏   . . . .
❏ ❏   . . . .

Sarah Kelling & Max Bittersohn

❏ ❏   1 - The Family Vault (1979)
❏ ❏   2 - The Withdrawing Room (1980)
❏ ❏   3 - The Palace Guard (1981)
❏ ❏   4 - The Bilbao Looking Glass (1983)
❏ ❏   5 - The Convivial Codfish (1984)
❏ ❏   6 - The Plain Old Man (1985)
❏ ❏   7 - The Recycled Citizen (1987)
❏ ❏   8 - The Silver Ghost (1987)
❏ ❏   9 - The Gladstone Bag (1989)
❏ ❏ 10 - The Resurrection Man (1992)
❏ ❏ 11 - The Odd Job (1995)
❏ ❏ 12 - The Balloon Man (1998)
❏ ❏   . . . .
❏ ❏   . . . .

MacPHERSON, Rett [P]

Torie O'Shea

❏ ❏   1 - Family Skeletons (1997)
❏ ❏   2 - A Veiled Antiquity (1998)
❏ ❏   . . . .
❏ ❏   . . . .

MAIMAN, Jaye

Robin Miller

❑ ❑   1 - I Left My Heart (1991)
❑ ❑   2 - Crazy for Loving (1992)★
❑ ❑   3 - Under My Skin (1993)
❑ ❑   4 - Someone to Watch (1995)
❑ ❑   5 - Baby It's Cold (1996)
❑ ❑   6 - Old Black Magic (1997)
❑ ❑   . . . .
❑ ❑   . . . .

MALMONT, Valerie S.

Tori Miracle

❑ ❑   1 - Death Pays the Rose Rent (1994)
❑ ❑   2 - Death, Lies and Apple Pies (1997)
❑ ❑   . . . .
❑ ❑   . . . .

MANEY, Mabel

Nancy Clue

❑ ❑   1 - The Case of the Not-So-Nice Nurse (1993)
❑ ❑   2 - The Case of the Good-for-Nothing Girlfriend
            (1994)
❑ ❑   3 - The Ghost in the Closet (1995)
❑ ❑   . . . .
❑ ❑   . . . .

MANN, Jessica

Tamara Hoyland

❑ ❑   1 - Funeral Sites (1982)
❑ ❑   2 - No Man's Island (1983)
❑ ❑   3 - Grave Goods (1984)
❑ ❑   4 - A Kind of Healthy Grave (1986)
❑ ❑   5 - Death Beyond the Nile (1988)
❑ ❑   6 - Faith, Hope and Homicide (1991)
❑ ❑   . . . .
❑ ❑   . . . .

Thea Crawford

❑ ❑   1 - The Only Security (1972)
❑ ❑   - U.S.-Troublecross
❑ ❑   2 - Captive Audience (1975)
❑ ❑   . . . .
❑ ❑   . . . .

MANTHORNE, Jackie

Elizabeth Ellis

❑ ❑   1 - Phantom of Queen Street (1999)
❑ ❑   . . . .
❑ ❑   . . . .

Harriet Hubbley

❑ ❑   1 - Ghost Motel (1994)
❑ ❑   2 - Deadly Reunion (1995)
❑ ❑   3 - Last Resort (1995)
❑ ❑   4 - Final Take (1996)
❑ ❑   5 - Sudden Death (1997)
❑ ❑   . . . .
❑ ❑   . . . .

MARACOTTA, Lindsay

Lucy Freers

❑ ❑   1 - The Dead Hollywood Moms Society (1996)
❑ ❑   2 - The Dead Celeb (1997)
❑ ❑   . . . .
❑ ❑   . . . .

MARCY, Jean

Meg Darcy

❑ ❑   1 - Cemetery Murders (1997)
❑ ❑   2 - Dead and Blonde (1998)
❑ ❑   . . . .
❑ ❑   . . . .

MARIZ, Linda French

Laura Ireland
❏ ❏   1 - Body English (1992)
❏ ❏   2 - Snake Dance (1992)
❏ ❏   . . . .
❏ ❏   . . . .

MARON, Margaret

Deborah Knott
❏ ❏   1 - Bootlegger's Daughter (1992)★★★★
❏ ❏   2 - Southern Discomfort (1993)☆☆
❏ ❏   3 - Shooting at Loons (1994)
❏ ❏   4 - Up Jumps the Devil (1996)★
❏ ❏   5 - Killer Market (1997)
❏ ❏   6 - Homefires Burning (1998)
❏ ❏   . . . .
❏ ❏   . . . .

Sigrid Harald
❏ ❏   1 - One Coffee With (1981)
❏ ❏   2 - Death of a Butterfly (1984)
❏ ❏   3 - Death in Blue Folders (1985)
❏ ❏   4 - The Right Jack (1987)
❏ ❏   5 - Baby Doll Games (1988)
❏ ❏   6 - Corpus Christmas (1989)☆☆☆
❏ ❏   7 - Past Imperfect (1991)
❏ ❏   8 - Fugitive Colors (1995)
❏ ❏   . . . .
❏ ❏   . . . .

MARTIN, Allana

Texana Jones
❏ ❏   1 - Death of a Healing Woman (1996)
❏ ❏   2 - Death of a Saint Maker (1998)
❏ ❏   3 - Death of an Evangelista (1999)
❏ ❏   . . . .
❏ ❏   . . . .

MARTIN, Lee [P]

Deb Ralston

❑ ❑   1 - Too Sane a Murder (1984)
❑ ❑   2 - A Conspiracy of Strangers (1986)
❑ ❑   3 - Death Warmed Over (1988)
❑ ❑   4 - Murder at the Blue Owl (1988)
❑ ❑   5 - Hal's Own Murder Case (1989)
❑ ❑   6 - Deficit Ending (1990)
❑ ❑   7 - The Mensa Murders (1990)
❑ ❑   8 - Hacker (1992)
❑ ❑   9 - The Day That Dusty Died (1993)
❑ ❑ 10 - Inherited Murder (1994)
❑ ❑ 11 - Bird in a Cage (1995)
❑ ❑ 12 - The Thursday Club (1997)
❑ ❑   . . . .
❑ ❑   . . . .

MASON, Sarah Jill

Trewley & Stone

❑ ❑   1 - Murder in the Maze (1993)
❑ ❑   2 - Frozen Stiff (1993)
❑ ❑   3 - Corpse in the Kitchen (1993)
❑ ❑   4 - Dying Breath (1994)
❑ ❑   5 - Sew Easy to Kill (1996)
❑ ❑   6 - Seeing Is Deceiving (1997)
❑ ❑   . . . .
❑ ❑   . . . .

MASSEY, Sujata

Rei Shimura

❑ ❑   1 - The Salaryman's Wife (1997)★☆
❑ ❑   2 - Zen Attitude (1998)
❑ ❑   3 - The Flower Master (1999)
❑ ❑   . . . .
❑ ❑   . . . .

MASTERS, Priscilla

Joanna Piercy

- ❏ ❏ 1 - Winding up the Serpent (1995)
- ❏ ❏ 2 - Catch the Fallen Sparrow (1996)
- ❏ ❏ 3 - A Wreath for My Sister (1997)
- ❏ ❏ 4 - And None Shall Sleep (1997)
- ❏ ❏ 5 - Scaring Crows (1999)
- ❏ ❏ . . . .
- ❏ ❏ . . . .

MATERA, Lia

Laura Di Palma

- ❏ ❏ 1 - The Smart Money (1988)
- ❏ ❏ 2 - The Good Fight (1990)☆
- ❏ ❏ 3 - A Hard Bargain (1992)
- ❏ ❏ 4 - Face Value (1994)
- ❏ ❏ 5 - Designer Crimes (1995)
- ❏ ❏ . . . .
- ❏ ❏ . . . .

Willa Jansson

- ❏ ❏ 1 - Where Lawyers Fear to Tread (1986)☆
- ❏ ❏ 2 - A Radical Departure (1987)☆☆
- ❏ ❏ 3 - Hidden Agenda (1989)
- ❏ ❏ 4 - Prior Convictions (1991)☆
- ❏ ❏ 5 - Last Chants (1996)
- ❏ ❏ 6 - Star Witness (1997)
- ❏ ❏ 7 - Havana Twist (1998)
- ❏ ❏ . . . .
- ❏ ❏ . . . .

MATHER, Linda

Jo Hughes

- ❏ ❏ 1 - Blood of an Aries (1994)
- ❏ ❏ 2 - Beware Taurus (1994)
- ❏ ❏ 3 - Gemini Doublecross (1995)
- ❏ ❏ . . . .
- ❏ ❏ . . . .

MATHEWS, Francine
Meredith Folger
❏ ❏   1 - Death in the Off-Season (1994)
❏ ❏   2 - Death in Rough Water (1995)
❏ ❏   3 - Death in a Mood Indigo (1997)
❏ ❏   . . . .
❏ ❏   . . . .

MATTESON, Stefanie
Charlotte Graham
❏ ❏   1 - Murder at the Spa (1990)
❏ ❏   2 - Murder on the Cliff (1991)
❏ ❏   3 - Murder at Teatime (1991)
❏ ❏   4 - Murder on the Silk Road (1992)
❏ ❏   5 - Murder at the Falls (1993)
❏ ❏   6 - Murder on High (1994)
❏ ❏   7 - Murder Among the Angels (1996)
❏ ❏   8 - Murder Under the Palms (1997)
❏ ❏   . . . .
❏ ❏   . . . .

MATTHEWS, Alex
Cassidy McCabe
❏ ❏   1 - Secret's Shadow (1996)
❏ ❏   2 - Satan's Silence (1997)
❏ ❏   3 - Vendetta's Victim (1998)
❏ ❏   . . . .
❏ ❏   . . . .

MATTHEWS, Patricia
Casey Farrel
❏ ❏   1 - The Scent of Fear (1992)
❏ ❏   2 - Vision of Death (1993)
❏ ❏   3 - Taste of Evil (1993)
❏ ❏   4 - The Sound of Murder (1994)
❏ ❏   5 - The Touch of Terror (1995)
❏ ❏   . . . .
❏ ❏   . . . .

MAXWELL, A. E. [P]
Fiddler & Fiora Flynn

- ❏ ❏   1 - Just Another Day in Paradise (1985)
- ❏ ❏   2 - The Frog and the Scorpion (1986)
- ❏ ❏   3 - Gatsby's Vineyard (1987)
- ❏ ❏   4 - Just Enough Light to Kill (1988)
- ❏ ❏   5 - The Art of Survival (1989)
- ❏ ❏   6 - Money Burns (1991)
- ❏ ❏   7 - The King of Nothing (1992)
- ❏ ❏   8 - Murder Hurts (1993)
- ❏ ❏   . . . .
- ❏ ❏   . . . .

McALLESTER, Melanie
Elizabeth Mendoza & Ashley Johnson

- ❏ ❏   1 - The Lessons (1994)
- ❏ ❏   2 - The Search (1996)
- ❏ ❏   . . . .
- ❏ ❏   . . . .

McCAFFERTY, Barbara Taylor and Beverly Taylor Herald
Bert & Nan Tatum

- ❏ ❏   1 - Double Murder (1996)
- ❏ ❏   2 - Double Exposure (1997)
- ❏ ❏   3 - Double Cross (1998)
- ❏ ❏   . . . .
- ❏ ❏   . . . .

McCAFFERTY, Jeanne
Mackenzie Griffin

- ❏ ❏   1 - Star Gazer (1994)
- ❏ ❏   2 - Artist Unknown (1995)
- ❏ ❏   3 - Finales & Overtures (1996)
- ❏ ❏   . . . .
- ❏ ❏   . . . .

McCAFFERTY, Taylor
Haskell Blevins
- ❏ ❏   1 - Pet Peeves (1990)
- ❏ ❏   2 - Ruffled Feathers (1992)
- ❏ ❏   3 - Bed Bugs (1992)
- ❏ ❏   4 - Thin Skins (1994)
- ❏ ❏   5 - Hanky Panky (1995)
- ❏ ❏   6 - Funny Money (1998)
- ❏ ❏   . . . .
- ❏ ❏   . . . .

McCLELLAN, Janet
Tru North
- ❏ ❏   1 - K. C. Bomber (1997)
- ❏ ❏   2 - Penn Valley Phoenix (1997)
- ❏ ❏   3 - River Quay (1998)
- ❏ ❏   . . . .
- ❏ ❏   . . . .

McCLELLAN, Tierney [P]
Schuyler Ridgway
- ❏ ❏   1 - Heir Condition (1995)
- ❏ ❏   2 - Closing Statement (1995)
- ❏ ❏   3 - A Killing in Real Estate (1996)
- ❏ ❏   4 - Two-Story Frame (1997)
- ❏ ❏   . . . .
- ❏ ❏   . . . .

McCLENDON, Lise
Alix Thorssen
- ❏ ❏   1 - The Bluejay Shaman (1994)
- ❏ ❏   2 - Painted Truth (1995)
- ❏ ❏   . . . .
- ❏ ❏   . . . .

McCONNELL, Vickie P.

Nyla Wade

❏ ❏   1 - Mrs. Porter's Letter (1982)
❏ ❏   2 - The Burnton Widows (1984)
❏ ❏   3 - Double Daughter (1988)
❏ ❏   . . . .
❏ ❏   . . . .

McCORMICK, Claire [P]

John Waltz

❏ ❏   1 - Resume for Murder (1982)
❏ ❏   2 - The Club Paradis Murders (1983)
❏ ❏   3 - Murder in Cowboy Bronze (1985)
❏ ❏   . . . .
❏ ❏   . . . .

McCRUMB, Sharyn

Elizabeth MacPherson

❏ ❏   1 - Sick of Shadows (1984)
❏ ❏   2 - Lovely in Her Bones (1985)
❏ ❏   3 - Highland Laddie Gone (1986)
❏ ❏   4 - Paying the Piper (1988)☆☆
❏ ❏   5 - The Windsor Knot (1990)
❏ ❏   6 - Missing Susan (1991)
❏ ❏   7 - MacPherson's Lament (1992)
❏ ❏   8 - If I'd Killed Him When I Met Him (1995)★
❏ ❏   . . . .
❏ ❏   . . . .

James Owens Mega

❏ ❏   1 - Bimbos of the Death Sun (1988)★☆
❏ ❏   2 - Zombies of the Gene Pool (1992)
❏ ❏   . . . .
❏ ❏   . . . .

Spencer Arrowood

- ❏ ❏ 1 - If Ever I Return, Pretty Peggy-O (1990)★☆
- ❏ ❏ 2 - The Hangman's Beautiful Daughter (1992)☆☆
- ❏ ❏ 3 - She Walks These Hills (1994)★★★
- ❏ ❏ 4 - The Rosewood Casket (1996)
- ❏ ❏ . . . .
- ❏ ❏ . . . .

McDERMID, Val

Kate Brannigan

- ❏ ❏ 1 - Dead Beat (1992)
- ❏ ❏ 2 - Kick Back (1993)
- ❏ ❏ 3 - Crack Down (1994)☆☆
- ❏ ❏ 4 - Clean Break (1995)
- ❏ ❏ 5 - Blue Genes (1996)
- ❏ ❏ 6 - Star Struck (1998)
- ❏ ❏ . . . .
- ❏ ❏ . . . .

Lindsay Gordon

- ❏ ❏ 1 - Report for Murder (1987)
- ❏ ❏ 2 - Common Murder (1989)
- ❏ ❏ 3 - Final Edition (1991)
- ❏ ❏ - U.S.-Open and Shut
- ❏ ❏ 4 - Union Jack (1993)
- ❏ ❏ 5 - Booked for Murder (1996)
- ❏ ❏ . . . .
- ❏ ❏ . . . .

Tony Hill & Carol Jordan

- ❏ ❏ 1 - The Mermaids Singing (1995)★
- ❏ ❏ 2 - The Wire in the Blood (1998)
- ❏ ❏ . . . .
- ❏ ❏ . . . .

McGIFFIN, Janet

Maxene St. Clair

- ❏ ❏ 1 - Emergency Murder (1992)
- ❏ ❏ 2 - Prescription for Death (1993)
- ❏ ❏ 3 - Elective Murder (1995)
- ❏ ❏ . . . .
- ❏ ❏ . . . .

McGOWN, Jill

Lloyd & Judy Hill

- ❑ ❑ 1 - A Perfect Match (1983)
- ❑ ❑ 2 - Redemption (1988)
- ❑ ❑   - U.S.-Murder at the Old Vicarage
- ❑ ❑ 3 - Death of a Dancer (1989)
- ❑ ❑   - U.S.-Gone to Her Death
- ❑ ❑ 4 - The Murders of Mrs. Austin & Mrs. Beale (1991)
- ❑ ❑ 5 - The Other Woman (1992)
- ❑ ❑ 6 - Murder Now and Then (1993)
- ❑ ❑ 7 - A Shred of Evidence (1995)
- ❑ ❑ 8 - Verdict Unsafe (1996)
- ❑ ❑ 9 - Picture of Innocence (1998)
- ❑ ❑ . . . .
- ❑ ❑ . . . .

McGUIRE, Christine

Kathryn Mackay

- ❑ ❑ 1 - Until Proven Guilty (1993)
- ❑ ❑ 2 - Until Justice is Done (1994)
- ❑ ❑ 3 - Until Death Do Us Part (1997)
- ❑ ❑ 4 - Until The Bough Breaks (1998)
- ❑ ❑ . . . .
- ❑ ❑ . . . .

McKENNA, Bridget

Caley Burke

- ❑ ❑ 1 - Murder Beach (1993)
- ❑ ❑ 2 - Dead Ahead (1994)☆
- ❑ ❑ 3 - Caught Dead (1995)
- ❑ ❑ . . . .
- ❑ ❑ . . . .

McKERNAN, Victoria

Chicago Nordejoong

- ❑ ❑ 1 - Osprey Reef (1990)
- ❑ ❑ 2 - Point Deception (1992)
- ❑ ❑ 3 - Crooked Island (1994)
- ❑ ❑ . . . .
- ❑ ❑ . . . .

McKEVETT, G. A. [P]
Savannah Reid
- ❏ ❏   1 - Just Desserts (1995)
- ❏ ❏   2 - Bitter Sweets (1996)
- ❏ ❏   3 - Killer Calories (1997)
- ❏ ❏   . . . .
- ❏ ❏   . . . .

McKITTERICK, Molly
Jennifer Burgess &
William Hecklepeck
- ❏ ❏   1 - The Medium is Murder (1992)
- ❏ ❏   2 - Murder in a Mayonnaise Jar (1993)
- ❏ ❏   . . . .
- ❏ ❏   . . . .

McNAB, Claire
Carol Ashton
- ❏ ❏   1 - Lessons in Murder (1988)
- ❏ ❏   2 - Fatal Reunion (1989)
- ❏ ❏   3 - Death Down Under (1990)
- ❏ ❏   4 - Cop Out (1991)
- ❏ ❏   5 - Dead Certain (1992)
- ❏ ❏   - APA-Off Key
- ❏ ❏   6 - Body Guard (1994)
- ❏ ❏   7 - Double Bluff (1995)
- ❏ ❏   8 - Inner Circle (1996)
- ❏ ❏   9 - Chain Letter (1997)
- ❏ ❏   10 - Past Due (1998)
- ❏ ❏   . . . .
- ❏ ❏   . . . .

McQUILLAN, Karin
Jazz Jasper
- ❏ ❏   1 - Deadly Safari (1990)
- ❏ ❏   2 - Elephants' Graveyard (1993)
- ❏ ❏   3 - The Cheetah Chase (1994)
- ❏ ❏   . . . .
- ❏ ❏   . . . .

McSHEA, Susanna Hofmann

Mildred Bennett et al

❏ ❏   1 - Hometown Heroes (1990)
❏ ❏   2 - The Pumpkin-Shell Wife (1992)
❏ ❏   3 - Ladybug, Ladybug (1994)
❏ ❏   ....
❏ ❏   ....

MEDAWAR, Mardi Oakley

Tay-bodal

❏ ❏   1 - Death at Rainy Mountain (1996)
❏ ❏   2 - Witch of the Palo Duro (1997)
❏ ❏   3 - Murder at Medicine Lodge (1999)
❏ ❏   ....
❏ ❏   ....

MEEK, M. R. D.

Lennox Kemp

❏ ❏   1 - With Flowers That Fell (1983)
❏ ❏   2 - Hang the Consequences (1984)
❏ ❏   3 - The Split Second (1985)
❏ ❏   4 - In Remembrance of Rose (1986)
❏ ❏   5 - A Worm of Doubt (1987)
❏ ❏   6 - A Mouthful of Sand (1988)
❏ ❏   7 - A Loose Connection (1989)
❏ ❏   8 - This Blessed Plot (1990)
❏ ❏   9 - Touch & Go (1993)
❏ ❏ 10 - Postscript to Murder (1996)
❏ ❏   ....
❏ ❏   ....

MEIER, Leslie

Lucy Stone

❏ ❏   1 - Mail-Order Murder (1993)
❏ ❏   2 - Tippy-Toe Murder (1994)
❏ ❏   3 - Trick or Treat Murder (1996)
❏ ❏   4 - Back to School Murder (1997)
❏ ❏   5 - Mistletoe Murder (1998)
❏ ❏   ....
❏ ❏   ....

MELVILLE, Jennie [P]
Charmian Daniels

❏ ❏   1 - Come Home and Be Killed (1962)
❏ ❏   2 - Burning Is a Substitute for Loving (1963)
❏ ❏   3 - Murderers' Houses (1964)
❏ ❏   4 - There Lies Your Love (1965)
❏ ❏   5 - Nell Alone (1966)
❏ ❏   6 - A Different Kind of Summer (1967)
❏ ❏   7 - A New Kind of Killer, An Old Kind of Death (1970)
❏ ❏   - APA-A New Kind of Killer
❏ ❏   8 - Murder Has a Pretty Face (1981)
❏ ❏   9 - Death in the Garden (1987)
❏ ❏   - U.S.-Murder in the Garden
❏ ❏ 10 - Windsor Red (1988)
❏ ❏ 11 - A Cure for Dying (1989)
❏ ❏ 12 - Witching Murder (1990)
❏ ❏ 13 - Making Good Blood (1990)
❏ ❏   - U.S.-Footsteps in the Blood
❏ ❏ 14 - Dead Set (1992)
❏ ❏ 15 - Whoever Has the Heart (1993)
❏ ❏ 16 - Baby Drop (1994)
❏ ❏   - U.S.-Death in the Family
❏ ❏ 17 - The Morbid Kitchen (1995)
❏ ❏ 18 - The Woman Who Was Not There (1996)
❏ ❏ 19 - Revengeful Death (1998)
❏ ❏   . . . .
❏ ❏   . . . .

MERCER, Judy
Ariel Gold

new

❏ ❏   1 - Fast Forward (1996)
❏ ❏   2 - Double Take (1997)
❏ ❏   3 - Split Image (1998)
❏ ❏   . . . .
❏ ❏   . . . .

MEREDITH, D. R.

Charles Matthews

❏ ❏   1 - The Sheriff & the Panhandle Murders (1984)
❏ ❏   2 - The Sheriff & the Branding Iron Murders (1985)
❏ ❏   3 - The Sheriff & the Folsom Man Murders (1987)
❏ ❏   4 - The Sheriff & the Pheasant Hunt Murders (1993)
❏ ❏   5 - The Homefront Murders (1995)
❏ ❏   . . . .
❏ ❏   . . . .

John Lloyd Branson & Lydia Fairchild

❏ ❏   1 - Murder by Impulse (1988)☆
❏ ❏   2 - Murder by Deception (1989)☆
❏ ❏   3 - Murder by Masquerade (1990)
❏ ❏   4 - Murder by Reference (1991)
❏ ❏   5 - Murder by Sacrilege (1993)
❏ ❏   . . . .
❏ ❏   . . . .

MEYERS, Annette

Olivia Brown

❏ ❏   1 - Free Love (1999)
❏ ❏   . . . .
❏ ❏   . . . .

Xenia Smith & Leslie Wetzon

❏ ❏   1 - The Big Killing (1989)
❏ ❏   2 - Tender Death (1990)
❏ ❏   3 - The Deadliest Option (1991)
❏ ❏   4 - Blood on the Street (1992)
❏ ❏   5 - Murder: The Musical (1993)
❏ ❏   6 - These Bones Were Made for Dancin' (1995)
❏ ❏   7 - The Groaning Board (1997)
❏ ❏   . . . .
❏ ❏   . . . .

MEYERS, Maan [P]

The Tonnemans

- ❏ ❏   1 - The Dutchman (1992)
- ❏ ❏   2 - The Kingsbridge Plot (1993)
- ❏ ❏   3 - The High Constable (1994)
- ❏ ❏   4 - The Dutchman's Dilemma (1995)
- ❏ ❏   5 - The House on Mulberry Street (1996)
- ❏ ❏   6 - The Lucifer Contract (1998)
- ❏ ❏   . . . .
- ❏ ❏   . . . .

MICHAELS, Barbara [P]

Georgetown house

- ❏ ❏   1 - Ammie, Come Home (1968)
- ❏ ❏   2 - Shattered Silk (1986)
- ❏ ❏   3 - Stitches in Time (1995)
- ❏ ❏   . . . .
- ❏ ❏   . . . .

MICHAELS, Melisa

Rosie Lavine

- ❏ ❏   1 - Cold Iron (1997)
- ❏ ❏   2 - Sister to the Rain (1998)
- ❏ ❏   . . . .
- ❏ ❏   . . . .

MICKELBURY, Penny

Carole Ann Gibson

- ❏ ❏   1 - One Must Wait (1998)
- ❏ ❏   2 - Where to Choose (1999)
- ❏ ❏   . . . .
- ❏ ❏   . . . .

Gianna Maglione & Mimi Patterson

- ❏ ❏   1 - Keeping Secrets (1994)
- ❏ ❏   2 - Night Songs (1995)
- ❏ ❏   . . . .
- ❏ ❏   . . . .

MIKULSKI, Barbara and Marylouise Oates

Norie Gorzack

❏ ❏ 1 - Capitol Offense (1996)
❏ ❏ 2 - Capitol Venture (1997)
❏ ❏ . . . .
❏ ❏ . . . .

MILES, Margaret

Charlotte Willett & Richard Longfellow

❏ ❏ 1 - A Wicked Way to Burn (1998)
❏ ❏ 2 - Too Soon for Flowers (1999)
❏ ❏ . . . .
❏ ❏ . . . .

MILLHISER, Marlys

Charlie Greene

❏ ❏ 1 - Murder at Moot Point (1992)
❏ ❏ 2 - Death of the Office Witch (1993)
❏ ❏ 3 - Murder in a Hot Flash (1995)
❏ ❏ 4 - It's Murder Going Home (1996)
❏ ❏ 5 - Nobody Dies in a Casino (1999)
❏ ❏ . . . .
❏ ❏ . . . .

MINICHINO, Camille

Gloria Lamerino

❏ ❏ 1 - The Hydrogen Murder (1997)
❏ ❏ 2 - The Helium Murder (1998)
❏ ❏ 3 - The Lithium Murder (1999)
❏ ❏ . . . .
❏ ❏ . . . .

MITCHELL, Kay

John Morrissey

❏ ❏ 1 - A Lively Form of Death (1990)
❏ ❏ 2 - In Stony Places (1991)
❏ ❏ 3 - A Strange Desire (1994)
❏ ❏   - U.S.-Roots of Evil

❏ ❏ 4 - A Portion for Foxes (1995)
❏ ❏ 5 - A Rage of Innocents (1996)
❏ ❏ . . . .
❏ ❏ . . . .

MOEN, Ruth Raby

Kathleen O'Shaughnessy

❏ ❏ 1 - Deadly Deceptions (1993)
❏ ❏ 2 - Only One Way Out (1994)
❏ ❏ 3 - Return to the Kill (1996)
❏ ❏ . . . .
❏ ❏ . . . .

MOFFAT, Gwen

Melinda Pink

❏ ❏ 1 - Lady With a Cool Eye (1973)
❏ ❏ 2 - Miss Pink at the Edge of the World (1975)
❏ ❏ 3 - Over the Sea to Death (1976)
❏ ❏ 4 - A Short Time to Live (1976)
❏ ❏ 5 - Persons Unknown (1978)
❏ ❏ 6 - The Buckskin Girl (1982)
❏ ❏ 7 - Miss Pink's Mistake (1982)
❏ ❏ 8 - Die Like a Dog (1982)
❏ ❏ 9 - Last Chance Country (1983)
❏ ❏ 10 - Grizzly Trail (1984)
❏ ❏ 11 - Snare (1987)
❏ ❏ 12 - The Stone Hawk (1989)
❏ ❏ 13 - Rage (1990)
❏ ❏ 14 - Veronica's Sisters (1992)
❏ ❏ . . . .
❏ ❏ . . . .

MONFREDO, Miriam Grace

Glynis Tryon

❏ ❏ 1 - Seneca Falls Inheritance (1992)☆☆
❏ ❏ 2 - North Star Conspiracy (1993)
❏ ❏ 3 - Blackwater Spirits (1995)
❏ ❏ 4 - Through a Gold Eagle (1996)
❏ ❏ 5 - Must the Maiden Die (1999)
❏ ❏ . . . .
❏ ❏ . . . .

MONTGOMERY, Yvonne E.

Finny Aletter

❑ ❑   1 - Scavengers (1987)
❑ ❑   2 - Obstacle Course (1990)
❑ ❑   . . . .
❑ ❑   . . . .

MOODY, Skye Kathleen

Venus Diamond

❑ ❑   1 - Rain Dance (1996)
❑ ❑   2 - Blue Poppy (1997)
❑ ❑   3 - Wildcrafters (1998)
❑ ❑   . . . .
❑ ❑   . . . .

MOODY, Susan

Cassandra Swann

❑ ❑   1 - Death Takes a Hand (1993)
❑ ❑   - Brit.-Takeout Double
❑ ❑   2 - Grand Slam (1994)
❑ ❑   3 - King of Hearts (1995)
❑ ❑   4 - Doubled in Spades (1996)
❑ ❑   5 - Sacrifice Bid (1997)
❑ ❑   6 - Dummy Hand (1998)
❑ ❑   . . . .
❑ ❑   . . . .

Penny Wanawake

❑ ❑   1 - Penny Black (1984)
❑ ❑   2 - Penny Dreadful (1984)
❑ ❑   3 - Penny Post (1985)
❑ ❑   4 - Penny Royal (1986)
❑ ❑   5 - Penny Wise (1988)
❑ ❑   6 - Penny Pinching (1989)
❑ ❑   7 - Penny Saving (1993)
❑ ❑   . . . .
❑ ❑   . . . .

MOORE, Barbara
Gordon Christy
- ❏ ❏ 1 - The Doberman Wore Black (1983)
- ❏ ❏ 2 - The Wolf Whispered Death (1986)
- ❏ ❏ . . . .
- ❏ ❏ . . . .

MOORE, Margaret
Richard Baxter
- ❏ ❏ 1 - Forests of the Night (1987)
- ❏ ❏ 2 - Dangerous Conceits (1988)
- ❏ ❏ 3 - Murder in Good Measure (1990)
- ❏ ❏ . . . .
- ❏ ❏ . . . .

MOORE, Miriam Ann
Marti Hirsch & Jerry Barlow
- ❏ ❏ 1 - Last Dance (1997)
- ❏ ❏ 2 - Stayin' Alive (1998)
- ❏ ❏ . . . .
- ❏ ❏ . . . .

MORELL, Mary
Lucia Ramos
- ❏ ❏ 1 - Final Session (1991)
- ❏ ❏ 2 - Final Rest (1993)
- ❏ ❏ . . . .
- ❏ ❏ . . . .

MORGAN, D. Miller
Daisy Marlow & Sam Milo
- ❏ ❏ 1 - Money Leads to Murder (1987)
- ❏ ❏   - APA-Rendezvous Kit Marlow
- ❏ ❏ 2 - A Lovely Night to Kill (1988)
- ❏ ❏ . . . .
- ❏ ❏ . . . .

MORGAN, Kate [P]

Dewey James

- ❏ ❏   1 - A Slay at the Races (1990)
- ❏ ❏   2 - Murder Most Fowl (1991)
- ❏ ❏   3 - Home Sweet Homicide (1992)
- ❏ ❏   4 - Mystery Loves Company (1992)
- ❏ ❏   5 - Days of Crime and Roses (1992)
- ❏ ❏   6 - Wanted Dude or Alive (1994)
- ❏ ❏   7 - Old School Dies (1996)
- ❏ ❏   . . . .
- ❏ ❏   . . . .

MORISON, B. J.

Elizabeth Lamb

- ❏ ❏   1 - Champagne and a Gardener (1982)
- ❏ ❏   2 - Port and a Star Border (1984)
- ❏ ❏   3 - Beer and Skittles (1985)
- ❏ ❏   4 - The Voyage of the Chianti (1987)
- ❏ ❏   5 - The Martini Effect (1992)
- ❏ ❏   . . . .
- ❏ ❏   . . . .

MORRONE, Wenda Wardell

new

Claude Willetts

- ❏ ❏   1 - Freefall in Cutthroat Gorge (2000)
- ❏ ❏   . . . .
- ❏ ❏   . . . .

Lorelei Muldoon

- ❏ ❏   1 - No Time For an Everyday Woman
  [incl Claude Willetts] (1997)
- ❏ ❏   2 - Millenium Bridges Falling Down (1999)
- ❏ ❏   . . . .
- ❏ ❏   . . . .

MOYES, Patricia
Henry & Emmy Tibbett
❏ ❏ 1 - Dead Men Don't Ski (1959)
❏ ❏ 2 - Down Among the Dead Men (1961)
❏ ❏ 3 - Death on the Agenda (1962)
❏ ❏ 4 - Murder a la Mode (1963)
❏ ❏ 5 - Falling Star (1964)
❏ ❏ 6 - Johnny Underground (1965)
❏ ❏ 7 - Murder Fantastical (1967)
❏ ❏ 8 - Death and the Dutch Uncle (1968)
❏ ❏ 9 - Many Deadly Returns (1970)☆
❏ ❏   - Brit.-Who Saw Her Die?
❏ ❏ 10 - Season of Snows and Sins (1971)
❏ ❏ 11 - The Curious Affair of the Third Dog (1973)
❏ ❏ 12 - Black Widower (1975)
❏ ❏ 13 - The Coconut Killings (1977)
❏ ❏ 14 - Who Is Simon Warwick? (1979)
❏ ❏ 15 - Angel Death (1980)
❏ ❏ 16 - A Six-Letter Word for Death (1983)
❏ ❏ 17 - Night Ferry to Death (1985)
❏ ❏ 18 - Black Girl, White Girl (1989)
❏ ❏ 19 - Twice in a Blue Moon (1993)
❏ ❏ . . . .
❏ ❏ . . . .

MULLER, Marcia
Elena Oliverez
❏ ❏ 1 - The Tree of Death (1983)
❏ ❏ 2 - The Legend of the Slain Soldiers (1985)
❏ ❏ 3 - Beyond the Grave (1986)
❏ ❏ . . . .
❏ ❏ . . . .

Joanna Stark
❏ ❏ 1 - The Cavalier in White (1986)
❏ ❏ 2 - There Hangs the Knife (1988)
❏ ❏ 3 - Dark Star (1989)
❏ ❏ . . . .
❏ ❏ . . . .

Sharon McCone

❑ ❑   1 - Edwin of the Iron Shoes (1977)
❑ ❑   2 - Ask the Cards a Question (1982)
❑ ❑   3 - The Cheshire Cat's Eye (1983)
❑ ❑   4 - Games to Keep the Dark Away (1984)
❑ ❑   5 - Leave a Message for Willie (1984)
❑ ❑   6 - Double [w/Bill Pronzini] (1984)
❑ ❑   7 - There's Nothing To Be Afraid Of (1985)
❑ ❑   8 - Eye of the Storm (1988)
❑ ❑   9 - There's Something in a Sunday (1989)
❑ ❑ 10 - The Shape of Dread (1989)★☆
❑ ❑ 11 - Trophies and Dead Things (1990)
❑ ❑ 12 - Where Echoes Live (1991)☆
❑ ❑ 13 - Pennies on a Dead Woman's Eyes (1992)
❑ ❑ 14 - Wolf in the Shadows (1993)★☆☆
❑ ❑ 15 - Till the Butchers Cut Him Down (1994)
❑ ❑ ss - The McCone Files (1995)
❑ ❑ 16 - A Wild and Lonely Place (1995)☆
❑ ❑ 17 - The Broken Promise Land (1996)
❑ ❑ 18 - Both Ends of the Night (1997)
❑ ❑ 19 - While Other People Sleep (1998)
❑ ❑ ss - McCone and Friends (1999)
❑ ❑ 20 - A Walk Through Fire (1999)
❑ ❑   . . . .
❑ ❑   . . . .

MUNGER, Katy

Casey Jones

❑ ❑   1 - Legwork (1997)☆
❑ ❑   2 - Out of Time (1998)
❑ ❑   . . . .
❑ ❑   . . . .

MURPHY, Shirley Rousseau

Joe Grey

❑ ❑   1 - Cat on the Edge (1996)
❑ ❑   2 - Cat Under Fire (1997)
❑ ❑   3 - Cat Raise the Dead (1997)
❑ ❑   4 - Cat in the Dark (1999)
❑ ❑   . . . .
❑ ❑   . . . .

MURRAY, Donna Huston

Ginger Struve Barnes

- ❏ ❏ 1 - The Main Line Is Murder (1995)
- ❏ ❏ 2 - Final Arrangements (1996)
- ❏ ❏ 3 - School of Hard Knocks (1997)
- ❏ ❏ 4 - No Bones About It (1998)
- ❏ ❏ 5 - Illegal Procedure (1998)
- ❏ ❏ . . . .
- ❏ ❏ . . . .

MURRAY, Lynne

Josephine Fuller

- ❏ ❏ 1 - Larger Than Death (1997)
- ❏ ❏ 2 - Large Target (1998)
- ❏ ❏ 3 - Lucille at Large (1999)
- ❏ ❏ 4 - A Ton of Trouble (2000)
- ❏ ❏ . . . .
- ❏ ❏ . . . .

MYERS, Amy

Auguste Didier

- ❏ ❏ 1 - Murder in Pug's Parlour (1986)
- ❏ ❏ 2 - Murder in the Limelight (1986)
- ❏ ❏ 3 - Murder at Plum's (1989)
- ❏ ❏ 4 - Murder at the Masque (1991)
- ❏ ❏ 5 - Murder Makes an Entree (1992)
- ❏ ❏ 6 - Murder Under the Kissing Bough (1992)
- ❏ ❏ 7 - Murder in the Smokehouse (1994)
- ❏ ❏ 8 - Murder at the Music Hall (1995)
- ❏ ❏ 9 - Murder in the Motor Stable (1996)
- ❏ ❏ . . . .
- ❏ ❏ . . . .

MYERS, Tamar

Abigail Timberlake

- ❏ ❏ 1 - Larceny and Old Lace (1996)
- ❏ ❏ 2 - Gilt by Association (1996)
- ❏ ❏ 3 - The Ming and I (1997)

❏ ❏ 4 - So Faux, So Good (1998)
❏ ❏ 5 - Baroque and Desperate (1999)
❏ ❏ 6 - Estate of Mind (1999)
❏ ❏ . . . .
❏ ❏ . . . .

Magdalena Yoder

❏ ❏ 1 - Too Many Crooks Spoil the Broth (1994)
❏ ❏ 2 - Parsley, Sage, Rosemary and Crime (1995)
❏ ❏ 3 - No Use Dying Over Spilled Milk (1996)
❏ ❏ 4 - Just Plain Pickled to Death (1997)
❏ ❏ 5 - Between a Wok and a Hard Place (1998)
❏ ❏ 6 - Eat, Drink and Be Wary (1998)
❏ ❏ 7 - Play It Again, Spam (1999)
❏ ❏ 8 - The Hand That Rocks the Ladle (1999)
❏ ❏ . . . .
❏ ❏ . . . .

NABB, Magdalen
Salvatore Guarnaccia
❑ ❑   1 - Death of an Englishman (1981)
❑ ❑   2 - Death of a Dutchman (1982)
❑ ❑   3 - Death in Springtime (1983)
❑ ❑   4 - Death in Autumn (1984)
❑ ❑   5 - The Marshal and the Murderer (1987)
❑ ❑   6 - The Marshal and the Madwoman (1988)
❑ ❑   7 - The Marshal's Own Case (1990)
❑ ❑   8 - The Marshal Makes His Report (1991)
❑ ❑   9 - The Marshal at the Villa Torrini (1993)
❑ ❑ 10 - The Marshal and the Forgery (1995)
❑ ❑   . . . .
❑ ❑   . . . .

NADELSON, Reggie
Artie Cohen
❑ ❑   1 - Red Hot Blues (1997)
❑ ❑   2 - Hot Poppies (1998)
❑ ❑   3 - Bloody Sunday (1999)
❑ ❑   . . . .
❑ ❑   . . . .

NAVRATILOVA, Martina and Liz Nickles
Jordan Myles
❑ ❑   1 - The Total Zone (1994)
❑ ❑   2 - Breaking Point (1996)
❑ ❑   3 - Killer Instinct (1997)
❑ ❑   . . . .
❑ ❑   . . . .

NEEL, Janet [P]
John McLeish & Francesca Wilson
❑ ❑   1 - Death's Bright Angel (1988)★
❑ ❑   2 - Death on Site (1989)
❑ ❑   3 - Death of a Partner (1991)

❏ ❏ 4 - Death Among the Dons (1993)☆
❏ ❏ 5 - A Timely Death (1996)
❏ ❏ 6 - To Die For (1998)
❏ ❏ . . . .
❏ ❏ . . . .

NEELY, Barbara
Blanche White

❏ ❏ 1 - Blanche on the Lam (1992)★★★
❏ ❏ 2 - Blanche Among the Talented Tenth (1994)
❏ ❏ 3 - Blanche in the 'Hood (1996)
❏ ❏ 4 - Blanche Cleans Up (1998)
❏ ❏ . . . .
❏ ❏ . . . .

NESSEN, Ron
and Johanna Neuman
Jerry Knight & Jane Day

❏ ❏ 1 - Knight and Day (1995)
❏ ❏ 2 - Press Corpse (1996)
❏ ❏ 3 - Death With Honors (1998)
❏ ❏ . . . .
❏ ❏ . . . .

NEWMAN, Sharan
Catherine LeVendeur

❏ ❏ 1 - Death Comes as Epiphany (1993)★☆☆
❏ ❏ 2 - The Devil's Door (1994)
❏ ❏ 3 - The Wandering Arm (1995)☆
❏ ❏ 4 - Strong as Death (1996)☆
❏ ❏ 5 - Cursed in the Blood (1998)
❏ ❏ . . . .
❏ ❏ . . . .

NIELSEN, Helen
Simon Drake
- ❏ ❏ 1 - Gold Coast Nocturne (1951)
- ❏ ❏   - Brit.-Murder by Proxy
- ❏ ❏ 2 - After Midnight (1966)
- ❏ ❏ 3 - A Killer in the Street (1967)
- ❏ ❏ 4 - The Darkest Hour (1969)
- ❏ ❏ 5 - The Severed Key (1973)
- ❏ ❏ 6 - The Brink of Murder (1976)
- ❏ ❏ . . . .
- ❏ ❏ . . . .

NILES, Chris
Sam Ridley
- ❏ ❏ 1 - Spike It (1997)
- ❏ ❏ 2 - Run Time (1998)
- ❏ ❏ . . . .
- ❏ ❏ . . . .

NORTH, Suzanne
Phoebe Fairfax
- ❏ ❏ 1 - Healthy, Wealthy & Dead (1994)☆
- ❏ ❏ 2 - Seeing is Deceiving (1996)
- ❏ ❏ 3 - Unnatural Selection (1999)
- ❏ ❏ . . . .
- ❏ ❏ . . . .

NUNNALLY, Tiina
Margit Andersson
- ❏ ❏ 1 - RuneMaker (1996)
- ❏ ❏ 2 - Fate of Ravens (1998)
- ❏ ❏ . . . .
- ❏ ❏ . . . .

O'BRIEN, Meg

Jessica James

❏ ❏   1 - The Daphne Decisions (1990)
❏ ❏   2 - Salmon in the Soup (1990)
❏ ❏   3 - Hare Today, Gone Tomorrow (1991)
❏ ❏   4 - Eagles Die Too (1992)
❏ ❏   5 - A Bright Flamingo Shroud (1997)
❏ ❏   . . . .
❏ ❏   . . . .

O'CALLAGHAN, Maxine

Anne Menlo

❏ ❏   1 - Shadow of a Child (1996)
❏ ❏   2 - Ashes to Ashes (1997)
❏ ❏   . . . .
❏ ❏   . . . .

Delilah West

❏ ❏   1 - Death Is Forever (1980)
❏ ❏   2 - Run From Nightmare (1981)
❏ ❏   3 - Hit and Run (1989)
❏ ❏   4 - Set-Up (1991)
❏ ❏   5 - Trade-Off (1994)
❏ ❏   6 - Down for the Count (1997)☆
❏ ❏   . . . .
❏ ❏   . . . .

O'CONNELL, Carol

Kathleen Mallory

❏ ❏   1 - Mallory's Oracle (1994)☆☆
❏ ❏   2 - The Man Who Cast Two Shadows (1995)
❏ ❏   3 - Killing Critics (1996)
❏ ❏   . . . .
❏ ❏   . . . .

O'DONNELL, Lillian

Gwenn Ramadge

- ❏ ❏ 1 - A Wreath for the Bride (1990)
- ❏ ❏ 2 - Used to Kill (1993)
- ❏ ❏ 3 - Raggedy Man (1995)
- ❏ ❏ 4 - The Goddess Affair (1997)
- ❏ ❏ . . . .
- ❏ ❏ . . . .

Mici Anhalt

- ❏ ❏ 1 - Aftershock (1977)
- ❏ ❏ 2 - Falling Star (1979)
- ❏ ❏ 3 - Wicked Designs (1980)
- ❏ ❏ . . . .
- ❏ ❏ . . . .

Norah Mulcahaney

- ❏ ❏ 1 - The Phone Calls (1972)
- ❏ ❏ 2 - Don't Wear Your Wedding Ring (1973)
- ❏ ❏ 3 - Dial 557 R-A-P-E (1974)
- ❏ ❏ 4 - The Baby Merchants (1975)
- ❏ ❏ 5 - Leisure Dying (1976)
- ❏ ❏ 6 - No Business Being a Cop (1979)
- ❏ ❏ 7 - The Children's Zoo (1981)
- ❏ ❏ 8 - Cop Without a Shield (1983)
- ❏ ❏ 9 - Ladykiller (1984)
- ❏ ❏ 10 - Casual Affairs (1985)
- ❏ ❏ 11 - The Other Side of the Door (1987)
- ❏ ❏ 12 - A Good Night to Kill (1989)
- ❏ ❏ 13 - A Private Crime (1991)
- ❏ ❏ 14 - Pushover (1992)
- ❏ ❏ 15 - Lockout (1994)
- ❏ ❏ 16 - Blue Death (1998)
- ❏ ❏ . . . .
- ❏ ❏ . . . .

O'KANE, Leslie

new

Allida Babcock

- ❏ ❏ 1 - Play Dead (1998)
- ❏ ❏ 2 - Wee Paws at a Murder (1999)
- ❏ ❏ . . . .
- ❏ ❏ . . . .

Molly Masters

❏ ❏ 1 - Death and Faxes (1996)
❏ ❏ 2 - Just the Fax Ma'am (1996)
❏ ❏ 3 - The Cold Hard Fax (1997)
❏ ❏ . . . .
❏ ❏ . . . .

O'MARIE, Carol Anne, Sister

Mary Helen, Sister

❏ ❏ 1 - A Novena for Murder (1984)
❏ ❏ 2 - Advent of Dying (1986)
❏ ❏ 3 - The Missing Madonna (1988)
❏ ❏ 4 - Murder in Ordinary Time (1991)
❏ ❏ 5 - Murder Makes a Pilgrimage (1993)
❏ ❏ 6 - Death Goes on Retreat (1995)
❏ ❏ 7 - Death of an Angel (1997)
❏ ❏ 8 - Death Takes Up a Collection (1998)
❏ ❏ . . . .
❏ ❏ . . . .

O'SHAUGHNESSY, Perri [P]

Nina Reilly

❏ ❏ 1 - Motion to Suppress (1995)
❏ ❏ 2 - Invasion of Privacy (1996)
❏ ❏ . . . .
❏ ❏ . . . .

OCORK, Shannon

Theresa Tracy Baldwin

❏ ❏ 1 - Sports Freak (1980)
❏ ❏ 2 - End of the Line (1981)
❏ ❏ 3 - Hell Bent for Heaven (1983)
❏ ❏ . . . .
❏ ❏ . . . .

OLEKSIW, Susan
Joe Silva
- ❑❑ 1 - Murder in Mellingham (1993)
- ❑❑ 2 - Double Take (1994)
- ❑❑ 3 - Family Album (1995)
- ❑❑ . . . .
- ❑❑ . . . .

OLIPHANT, B. J. [P]
Shirley McClintock
- ❑❑ 1 - Dead in the Scrub (1990)☆☆
- ❑❑ 2 - The Unexpected Corpse (1990)
- ❑❑ 3 - Deservedly Dead (1992)
- ❑❑ 4 - Death and the Delinquent (1992)
- ❑❑ 5 - Death Served up Cold (1994)
- ❑❑ 6 - A Ceremonial Death (1996)
- ❑❑ . . . .
- ❑❑ . . . .

OLIVER, Maria Antonia
Lonia Gulu
- ❑❑ 1 - A Study in Lilac (1987)
- ❑❑ 2 - Antipodes (1989)
- ❑❑ . . . .
- ❑❑ . . . .

ORDE, A. J. [P]
Jason Lynx
- ❑❑ 1 - A Little Neighborhood Murder (1989)
- ❑❑ 2 - Death and the Dogwalker (1990)
- ❑❑ 3 - Death for Old Times' Sake (1992)
- ❑❑ 4 - Looking for the Aardvark (1993)
- ❑❑   - APA-Dead on Sunday
- ❑❑ 5 - A Long Time Dead (1995)
- ❑❑ 6 - A Death of Innocents (1997)
- ❑❑ . . . .
- ❑❑ . . . .

OSBORNE, Denise

Queenie Davilov

❏ ❏   1 - Murder Offscreen (1994)
❏ ❏   2 - Cut to: Murder (1995)
❏ ❏   . . . .
❏ ❏   . . . .

PADGETT, Abigail

Barbara Joan "Bo" Bradley

- ❑ ❑ 1 - Child of Silence (1993)☆☆
- ❑ ❑ 2 - Strawgirl (1994)
- ❑ ❑ 3 - Turtle Baby (1995)
- ❑ ❑ 4 - Moonbird Boy (1996)
- ❑ ❑ 5 - The Dollmaker's Daughters (1997)
- ❑ ❑ . . . .
- ❑ ❑ . . . .

Blue McCarron

- ❑ ❑ 1 - Blue (1998)
- ❑ ❑ 2 - The Last Blue Plate Special (1999)
- ❑ ❑ . . . .
- ❑ ❑ . . . .

PAGE, Emma [P]

Kelsey, Insp.

- ❑ ❑ 1 - Missing Woman (1980)
- ❑ ❑ 2 - Every Second Thursday (1981)
- ❑ ❑ 3 - Last Walk Home (1982)
- ❑ ❑ 4 - Cold Light of Day (1983)
- ❑ ❑ 5 - Scent of Death (1985)
- ❑ ❑ 6 - Final Moments (1987)
- ❑ ❑ 7 - A Violent End (1988)
- ❑ ❑ 8 - Murder Comes Calling (1995)
- ❑ ❑ 9 - Intent to Kill (1998)
- ❑ ❑ . . . .
- ❑ ❑ . . . .

PAGE, Katherine Hall

Faith Sibley Fairchild

- ❑ ❑ 1 - The Body in the Belfry (1990)★
- ❑ ❑ 2 - The Body in the Kelp (1991)
- ❑ ❑ 3 - The Body in the Bouillon (1991)
- ❑ ❑ 4 - The Body in the Vestibule (1992)
- ❑ ❑ 5 - The Body in the Cast (1993)

❏ ❏   6 - The Body in the Basement (1994)
❏ ❏   7 - The Body in the Bog (1996)
❏ ❏   8 - The Body in the Fjord (1997)
❏ ❏   9 - The Body in the Bookcase (1998)
❏ ❏   . . . .
❏ ❏   . . . .

PAIGE, Robin [P]

Kathryn Ardleigh

❏ ❏   1 - Death at Bishop's Keep (1994)
❏ ❏   2 - Death at Gallows Green (1995)
❏ ❏   3 - Death at Daisy's Folly (1997)
❏ ❏   4 - Death at Devil's Bridge (1998)
❏ ❏   5 - Death at Rottingdean (1999)
❏ ❏   . . . .
❏ ❏   . . . .

PAPAZOGLOU, Orania

Patience Campbell McKenna

❏ ❏   1 - Sweet, Savage Death (1984)☆
❏ ❏   2 - Wicked, Loving Murder (1985)
❏ ❏   3 - Death's Savage Passion (1986)
❏ ❏   4 - Rich, Radiant Slaughter (1988)
❏ ❏   5 - Once and Always Murder (1990)
❏ ❏   . . . .
❏ ❏   . . . .

PARETSKY, Sara

V. I. Warshawski

❏ ❏   1 - Indemnity Only (1982)
❏ ❏   2 - Deadlock (1984)
❏ ❏   3 - Killing Orders (1985)
❏ ❏   4 - Bitter Medicine (1987)
❏ ❏   5 - Blood Shot (1988)★☆☆
❏ ❏   - Brit.-Toxic Shock
❏ ❏   6 - Burn Marks (1990)
❏ ❏   7 - Guardian Angel (1991)
❏ ❏   8 - Tunnel Vision (1994)
❏ ❏   ss - Windy City Blues [short stories] (1995)
❏ ❏   . . . .
❏ ❏   . . . .

PARKER, Barbara

Gail Connor

❏ ❏ 1 - Suspicion of Innocence (1994)☆
❏ ❏ 2 - Suspicion of Guilt (1995)
❏ ❏ 3 - Suspicion of Deceit (1998)
❏ ❏ ....
❏ ❏ ....

PATON Walsh, Jill

Imogen Quy

❏ ❏ 1 - The Wyndham Case (1993)
❏ ❏ 2 - A Piece of Justice (1995)☆
❏ ❏ ....
❏ ❏ ....

PAUL, Barbara

Enrico Caruso

❏ ❏ 1 - A Cadenza for Caruso [1910] (1984)
❏ ❏ 2 - Prima Donna at Large [1915] (1985)
❏ ❏ 3 - A Chorus of Detectives [1920] (1987)
❏ ❏ ....
❏ ❏ ....

Marian Larch

❏ ❏ 1 - The Renewable Virgin (1984)
❏ ❏ 2 - He Huffed and He Puffed (1989)
❏ ❏ 3 - Good King Sauerkraut (1989)
❏ ❏ 4 - You Have the Right to Remain Silent (1992)
❏ ❏ 5 - The Apostrophe Thief (1993)
❏ ❏ 6 - Fare Play (1995)
❏ ❏ 7 - Full Frontal Murder (1997)
❏ ❏ ....
❏ ❏ ....

PEART, Jane

Edgecliffe Manor Series

- ❑ ❑   1 - Web of Deception (1996)
- ❑ ❑   2 - Shadow of Fear (1996)
- ❑ ❑   3 - A Perilous Bargain (1997)
- ❑ ❑   4 - Thread of Suspicion (1998)
- ❑ ❑   ....
- ❑ ❑   ....

PENCE, Joanne

Angelina Amalfi

- ❑ ❑   1 - Something's Cooking (1993)
- ❑ ❑   2 - Too Many Cooks (1994)
- ❑ ❑   3 - Cooking up Trouble (1995)
- ❑ ❑   4 - Cooking Most Deadly (1996)
- ❑ ❑   5 - Cook's Night Out (1998)
- ❑ ❑   6 - Cooks Overboard (1998)
- ❑ ❑   ....
- ❑ ❑   ....

PENMAN, Sharon Kay

Justin de Quincy

- ❑ ❑   1 - The Queen's Man (1996)☆
- ❑ ❑   2 - Cruel as the Grave (1998)
- ❑ ❑   ....
- ❑ ❑   ....

PENN, John [P]

George Thorne

- ❑ ❑   1 - A Will to Kill (1983)
- ❑ ❑   2 - Mortal Term (1984)
- ❑ ❑   3 - A Deadly Sickness (1985)
- ❑ ❑   4 - Unto the Grave (1986)
- ❑ ❑   5 - Barren Revenge (1986)
- ❑ ❑   6 - Accident Prone (1987)
- ❑ ❑   ....
- ❑ ❑   ....

Richard Tansey
- ❑ ❑ 1 - A Feast of Death (1989)
- ❑ ❑ 2 - A Killing to Hide (1990)
- ❑ ❑ 3 - A Knife Ill-Used (1991)
- ❑ ❑ 4 - Death's Long Shadow (1991)
- ❑ ❑ 5 - So Many Steps to Death (1995)
- ❑ ❑ . . . .
- ❑ ❑ . . . .

PERRY, Anne
Thomas & Charlotte Pitt
- ❑ ❑ 1 - The Cater Street Hangman (1979)
- ❑ ❑ 2 - Callander Square (1980)
- ❑ ❑ 3 - Paragon Walk (1981)
- ❑ ❑ 4 - Resurrection Row (1981)
- ❑ ❑ 5 - Rutland Place (1983)
- ❑ ❑ 6 - Bluegate Fields (1984)
- ❑ ❑ 7 - Death in Devil's Acre (1985)
- ❑ ❑ 8 - Cardington Crescent (1987)
- ❑ ❑ 9 - Silence in Hanover Close (1988)
- ❑ ❑ 10 - Bethlehem Road (1990)
- ❑ ❑ 11 - Highgate Rise (1991)
- ❑ ❑ 12 - Belgrave Square (1992)
- ❑ ❑ 13 - Farrier's Lane (1993)
- ❑ ❑ 14 - The Hyde Park Headsman (1994)
- ❑ ❑ 15 - Traitor's Gate (1995)
- ❑ ❑ 16 - Pentecost Alley (1996)
- ❑ ❑ 17 - Ashworth Hall (1997)
- ❑ ❑ 18 - Brunswick Gardens (1998)
- ❑ ❑ . . . .
- ❑ ❑ . . . .

William Monk
- ❑ ❑ 1 - The Face of a Stranger (1990)☆
- ❑ ❑ 2 - A Dangerous Mourning (1991)
- ❑ ❑ 3 - Defend and Betray (1992)☆
- ❑ ❑ 4 - A Sudden, Fearful Death (1993)
- ❑ ❑ 5 - Sins of the Wolf (1994)
- ❑ ❑ 6 - Cain His Brother (1995)

❏ ❏   7 - Weighed in the Balance (1996)
❏ ❏   8 - The Silent Cry (1997)
❏ ❏   9 - A Breach of Promise (1998)
❏ ❏   . . . .
❏ ❏   . . . .

PETERS, Elizabeth [P]

Amelia Peabody

❏ ❏   1 - Crocodile on the Sandbank (1975)
❏ ❏   2 - The Curse of the Pharaohs (1981)
❏ ❏   3 - The Mummy Case (1985)
❏ ❏   4 - Lion in the Valley (1986)
❏ ❏   5 - The Deeds of the Disturber (1988)
❏ ❏   6 - The Last Camel Died at Noon (1991)☆
❏ ❏   7 - The Snake, the Crocodile and the Dog (1992)☆
❏ ❏   8 - The Hippopotamus Pool (1996)
❏ ❏   9 - Seeing a Large Cat (1997)☆
❏ ❏ 10 - The Ape Who Guards the Balance (1998)
❏ ❏ 11 - Serpent on Your Brow (1999)
❏ ❏ 12 - Thunder in the Sky (2000)
❏ ❏   . . . .
❏ ❏   . . . .

Jacqueline Kirby

❏ ❏   1 - The Seventh Sinner (1972)
❏ ❏   2 - The Murders of Richard III (1974)
❏ ❏   3 - Die for Love (1984)
❏ ❏   4 - Naked Once More (1989)★
❏ ❏   . . . .
❏ ❏   . . . .

Vicky Bliss

❏ ❏   1 - Borrower of the Night (1973)
❏ ❏   2 - Street of the Five Moons (1978)
❏ ❏   3 - Silhouette in Scarlet (1983)
❏ ❏   4 - Trojan Gold (1987)☆
❏ ❏   5 - Night Train to Memphis (1994)☆
❏ ❏   . . . .
❏ ❏   . . . .

PETERSON, Audrey [P]

Claire Camden

- ❏ ❏ 1 - Dartmoor Burial (1992)
- ❏ ❏ 2 - Death Too Soon (1994)
- ❏ ❏ 3 - Shroud for a Scholar (1995)
- ❏ ❏ ....
- ❏ ❏ ....

Jane Winfield

- ❏ ❏ 1 - The Nocturne Murder (1988)
- ❏ ❏ 2 - Death in Wessex (1989)
- ❏ ❏ 3 - Murder in Burgundy (1989)
- ❏ ❏ 4 - Deadly Rehearsal (1990)
- ❏ ❏ 5 - Elegy in a Country Graveyard (1990)
- ❏ ❏ 6 - Lament for Christabel (1991)
- ❏ ❏ ....
- ❏ ❏ ....

PETIT, Diane

Kathryn Bogert

- ❏ ❏ 1 - Goodbye Charli (1997)
- ❏ ❏ 2 - Take Two (1998)
- ❏ ❏ 3 - Third Time's A Charm (1999)
- ❏ ❏ ....
- ❏ ❏ ....

PETRIE, Rhona [P]

Marcus MacLurg

- ❏ ❏ 1 - Death in Deakins Wood (1963)
- ❏ ❏ 2 - Murder by Precedent (1964)
- ❏ ❏ 3 - Running Deep (1965)
- ❏ ❏ 4 - Dead Loss (1966)
- ❏ ❏ 5 - MacLurg Goes West (1968)
- ❏ ❏ ....
- ❏ ❏ ....

Nassim Pride

- ❏ ❏ 1 - Foreign Bodies (1967)
- ❏ ❏ 2 - Despatch of a Dove (1969)
- ❏ ❏ ....
- ❏ ❏ ....

PICKARD, Nancy

Eugenia Potter

❑ ❑   1 - The Cooking School Murders
          [by Virginia Rich] (1982)
❑ ❑   2 - The Baked Bean Supper Murders
          [by Virginia Rich] (1983)
❑ ❑   3 - The Nantucket Diet Murders
          [by Virginia Rich] (1985)
❑ ❑   4 - The 27-Ingredient Chile Con Carne Murders
          [with Virginia Rich] (1993)
❑ ❑   5 - The Blue Corn Murders (1998)
❑ ❑   . . . .
❑ ❑   . . . .

Jenny Cain

❑ ❑   1 - Generous Death (1984)
❑ ❑   2 - Say No to Murder (1985)★
❑ ❑   3 - No Body (1986)☆
❑ ❑   4 - Marriage Is Murder (1987)★☆
❑ ❑   5 - Dead Crazy (1988)☆☆
❑ ❑   6 - Bum Steer (1989)★
❑ ❑   7 - I. O. U. (1991)★★☆☆
❑ ❑   8 - But I Wouldn't Want to Die There (1993)
❑ ❑   9 - Confession (1994)
❑ ❑ 10 - Twilight (1995)☆
❑ ❑   . . . .
❑ ❑   . . . .

PIESMAN, Marissa

Nina Fischman

❑ ❑   1 - Unorthodox Practices (1989)
❑ ❑   2 - Personal Effects (1991)
❑ ❑   3 - Heading Uptown (1993)
❑ ❑   4 - Close Quarters (1994)
❑ ❑   5 - Alternate Sides (1995)
❑ ❑   6 - Survival Instincts (1997)
❑ ❑   . . . .
❑ ❑   . . . .

PINCUS, Elizabeth

Nell Fury

❏ ❏   1 - The Two-Bit Tango (1992)★
❏ ❏   2 - The Solitary Twist (1993)
❏ ❏   3 - The Hangdog Hustle (1995)
❏ ❏   . . . .
❏ ❏   . . . .

PORTER, Anna

Judith Hayes

❏ ❏   1 - Hidden Agenda (1985)
❏ ❏   2 - Mortal Sins (1987)
❏ ❏   . . . .
❏ ❏   . . . .

POWELL, Deborah

Hollis Carpenter

❏ ❏   1 - Bayou City Streets (1991)
❏ ❏   2 - Houston Town (1992)
❏ ❏   . . . .
❏ ❏   . . . .

PROWELL, Sandra West

Phoebe Siegel

❏ ❏   1 - By Evil Means (1993)☆☆
❏ ❏   2 - The Killing of Monday Brown (1994)☆
❏ ❏   3 - When Wallflowers Die (1996)
❏ ❏   . . . .
❏ ❏   . . . .

PUGH, Dianne G.

Iris Thorne

❏ ❏   1 - Cold Call (1993)
❏ ❏   2 - Slow Squeeze (1994)
❏ ❏   3 - Body Blow (1996)
❏ ❏   4 - Fast Friends (1997)
❏ ❏   . . . .
❏ ❏   . . . .

PULVER, Mary Monica

Peter & Kori Price Brichter

❏ ❏   1 - Murder at the War (1987)☆

❏ ❏   - APA-Knight Fall

❏ ❏   2 - The Unforgiving Minutes [prequel] (1988)

❏ ❏   3 - Ashes to Ashes (1988)

❏ ❏   4 - Original Sin (1991)

❏ ❏   5 - Show Stopper (1992)

❏ ❏   . . . .

❏ ❏   . . . .

QUEST, Erica [P]
Kate Maddox
- ❏ ❏   1 - Death Walk (1988)
- ❏ ❏   2 - Cold Coffin (1990)
- ❏ ❏   3 - Model Murder (1991)
- ❏ ❏   . . . .
- ❏ ❏   . . . .

QUINN, Elizabeth
Lauren Maxwell
- ❏ ❏   1 - Murder Most Grizzly (1993)
- ❏ ❏   2 - A Wolf in Death's Clothing (1995)
- ❏ ❏   3 - Lamb to the Slaughter (1996)
- ❏ ❏   4 - Killer Whale (1997)
- ❏ ❏   5 - Dead by a Whisker (1999)
- ❏ ❏   . . . .
- ❏ ❏   . . . .

QUINTON, Ann
James Roland & Patrick Mansfield
- ❏ ❏   1 - To Mourn a Mischief (1989)
- ❏ ❏   2 - Death of a Dear Friend (1990)
- ❏ ❏   3 - A Fatal End (1992)
- ❏ ❏   4 - A Little Grave (1994)
- ❏ ❏   5 - The Sleeping and the Dead (1994)
- ❏ ❏   6 - Some Foul Play (1997)
- ❏ ❏   . . . .
- ❏ ❏   . . . .

RADLEY, Sheila [P]

Douglas Quantrill & Hilary Lloyd

- ❏ ❏ 1 - Death and the Maiden (1978)
- ❏ ❏   - U.S.-Death in the Morning
- ❏ ❏ 2 - The Chief Inspector's Daughter (1980)
- ❏ ❏ 3 - A Talent for Destruction (1982)
- ❏ ❏ 4 - Blood on the Happy Highway (1983)
- ❏ ❏   - U.S.-The Quiet Road to Death
- ❏ ❏ 5 - Fate Worse Than Death (1985)
- ❏ ❏ 6 - Who Saw Him Die? (1987)
- ❏ ❏ 7 - This Way Out (1989)
- ❏ ❏ 8 - Cross My Heart and Hope to Die (1992)
- ❏ ❏ 9 - Fair Game (1994)
- ❏ ❏ ss - New Blood From Old Bones [short stories] (1998)
- ❏ ❏ . . . .
- ❏ ❏ . . . .

RAWLINGS, Ellen

Rachel Crowne

- ❏ ❏ 1 - The Murder Lover (1997)
- ❏ ❏ 2 - Deadly Harvest (1997)
- ❏ ❏ . . . .
- ❏ ❏ . . . .

RAYNER, Claire

George Barnabas

- ❏ ❏ 1 - First Blood (1993)
- ❏ ❏ 2 - Second Opinion (1994)
- ❏ ❏ 3 - Third Degree (1995)
- ❏ ❏ 4 - Fourth Attempt (1996)
- ❏ ❏ . . . .
- ❏ ❏ . . . .

REDMANN, J. M.

Michelle 'Micky' Knight

- ❏ ❏ 1 - Death by the Riverside (1990)
- ❏ ❏ 2 - Deaths of Jocasta (1993)
- ❏ ❏ 3 - The Intersection of Law and Desire (1995)★
- ❏ ❏ . . . .
- ❏ ❏ . . . .

REICHS, Kathleen

Temperance Brennan

- ❑ ❑ 1 - Déjà Dead (1997)
- ❑ ❑ 2 - Death du Jour (1999)
- ❑ ❑ ....
- ❑ ❑ ....

RENDELL, Ruth

Reginald Wexford

- ❑ ❑ 1 - From Doon With Death (1964)
- ❑ ❑ 2 - A Wolf to Slaughter (1967)
- ❑ ❑ 3 - A New Lease of Death (1967)
- ❑ ❑   - APA-Sins of the Fathers (1970)
- ❑ ❑ 4 - The Best Man to Die (1969)
- ❑ ❑ 5 - A Guilty Thing Surprised (1970)
- ❑ ❑ 6 - No More Dying Then (1971)
- ❑ ❑ 7 - Murder Being Once Done (1972)
- ❑ ❑ 8 - Some Lie and Some Die (1973)
- ❑ ❑ 9 - Shake Hands Forever (1975)
- ❑ ❑ 10 - A Sleeping Life (1978)☆
- ❑ ❑ 11 - Put on by Cunning (1981)
- ❑ ❑   - U.S.-Death Notes
- ❑ ❑ 12 - The Speaker of Mandarin (1983)
- ❑ ❑ 13 - An Unkindness of Ravens (1985)☆
- ❑ ❑ 14 - The Veiled One (1988)
- ❑ ❑ 15 - Kissing the Gunner's Daughter (1993)
- ❑ ❑ 16 - Simisola (1994)
- ❑ ❑ 17 - Road Rage (1997)
- ❑ ❑ ....
- ❑ ❑ ....

REUBEN, Shelly

Wylie Nolan & Max Bramble

- ❑ ❑ 1 - Origin and Cause (1994)
- ❑ ❑ 2 - Spent Matches (1996)
- ❑ ❑ ....
- ❑ ❑ ....

RICHARDSON, Tracey

Stevie Houston

❏ ❏   1 - Last Rites (1997)
❏ ❏   2 - Over the Line (1998)
❏ ❏   3 - Double Takeout (1998)
❏ ❏   . . . .
❏ ❏   . . . .

RICHMAN, Phyllis

Chas Wheatley

❏ ❏   1 - The Butter Did It (1997)☆
❏ ❏   2 - Murder on the Gravy Train (1999)
❏ ❏   . . . .
❏ ❏   . . . .

RIPLEY, Ann

Louise Eldridge

❏ ❏   1 - Mulch (1994)
❏ ❏   2 - Death of a Garden Pest (1996)
❏ ❏   3 - Death of a Political Plant (1998)
❏ ❏   . . . .
❏ ❏   . . . .

RIPPON, Marion

Maurice Ygrec

❏ ❏   1 - The Hand of Solange (1969)
❏ ❏   2 - Behold, the Druid Weeps (1970)
❏ ❏   3 - The Ninth Tentacle (1974)
❏ ❏   4 - Lucien's Tomb (1979)
❏ ❏   . . . .
❏ ❏   . . . .

ROBB, Candace M.

Owen Archer

❏ ❏   1 - The Apothecary Rose (1993)
❏ ❏   2 - The Lady Chapel (1994)
❏ ❏   3 - The Nun's Tale (1995)
❏ ❏   4 - The King's Bishop (1996)

❏ ❏   5 - The Riddle of St. Leonard's (1996)
❏ ❏   6 - A Gift of Sanctuary (1998)
❏ ❏   . . . .
❏ ❏   . . . .

ROBB, J. D. [P]
Eve Dallas
❏ ❏   1 - Naked in Death (1995)
❏ ❏   2 - Glory in Death (1996)
❏ ❏   3 - Immortal in Death (1996)
❏ ❏   4 - Rapture in Death (1996)
❏ ❏   5 - Ceremony in Death (1997)
❏ ❏   6 - Vengeance in Death (1997)
❏ ❏   7 - Holiday in Death (1998)
❏ ❏   8 - Conspiracy in Death (1999)
❏ ❏   . . . .
❏ ❏   . . . .

ROBERTS, Carey
Anne Fitzhugh
❏ ❏   1 - Touch a Cold Door (1989)
❏ ❏   2 - Pray God to Die (1993)
❏ ❏   . . . .
❏ ❏   . . . .

ROBERTS, Gillian [P]
Amanda Pepper
❏ ❏   1 - Caught Dead in Philadelphia (1987)★
❏ ❏   2 - Philly Stakes (1989)☆
❏ ❏   3 - I'd Rather Be in Philadelphia (1991)
❏ ❏   4 - With Friends Like These (1993)
❏ ❏   5 - How I Spent My Summer Vacation (1994)
❏ ❏   6 - In the Dead of Summer (1995)
❏ ❏   7 - The Mummers' Curse (1996)
❏ ❏   8 - The Bluest Blood (1998)
❏ ❏   . . . .
❏ ❏   . . . .

Emma Howe & Billie August

❑ ❑   1 - Time and Trouble (1998)

❑ ❑   . . . .

❑ ❑   . . . .

ROBERTS, Lillian M.

Andi Pauling

❑ ❑   1 - Riding for a Fall (1996)☆

❑ ❑   2 - The Hand That Feeds You (1997)

❑ ❑   3 - Almost Human (1998)

❑ ❑   . . . .

❑ ❑   . . . .

ROBERTS, Lora

Liz Sullivan

❑ ❑   1 - Murder in a Nice Neighborhood (1994)

❑ ❑   2 - Murder in the Marketplace (1995)

❑ ❑   3 - Murder Mile-High (1996)

❑ ❑   4 - Murder Bone by Bone (1997)

❑ ❑   5 - Murder Crops Up (1998)

❑ ❑   6 - Murder Follows Money (1999)

❑ ❑   . . . .

❑ ❑   . . . .

ROBINSON, Leah Ruth

Evelyn Sutcliffe

❑ ❑   1 - Blood Run [revised 1999] (1988)

❑ ❑   2 - First Cut (1998)

❑ ❑   . . . .

❑ ❑   . . . .

ROBINSON, Lynda S.

Lord Meren

❑ ❑   1 - Murder in the Place of Anubis (1994)

❑ ❑   2 - Murder at the God's Gate (1995)

❑ ❑   3 - Murder at the Feast of Rejoicing (1996)

❑ ❑   4 - Eater of Souls (1997)

❑ ❑   5 - Drinker of Blood (1998)

❑ ❑   . . . .

❑ ❑   . . . .

ROBITAILLE, Julie

Kit Powell

❏ ❏ 1 - Jinx (1992)
❏ ❏ 2 - Iced (1994)
❏ ❏ . . . .
❏ ❏ . . . .

ROE, Caroline [P]

Isaac & Bishop Berenguer

❏ ❏ 1 - Remedy for Treason (1998)
❏ ❏ 2 - Cure for a Charlatan (1999)
❏ ❏ 3 - Salve for a Sore Conscience (2000)
❏ ❏ . . . .
❏ ❏ . . . .

ROGERS, Chris

Dixie Flannigan

❏ ❏ 1 - Bitch Factor (1998)
❏ ❏ 2 - Rage Factor (1999)
❏ ❏ . . . .
❏ ❏ . . . .

ROGOW, Roberta

Charles Dodgson & Conan Doyle

❏ ❏ 1 - The Problem of the Missing Miss (1998)
❏ ❏ 2 - The Problem of the Spurious Spiritualist (1999)
❏ ❏ . . . .
❏ ❏ . . . .

ROMBERG, Nina

Marian Winchester

❏ ❏ 1 - The Spirit Stalker (1989)
❏ ❏ 2 - Shadow Walkers (1993)
❏ ❏ . . . .
❏ ❏ . . . .

ROOME, Annette
Christine Martin

❑ ❑   1 - A Real Shot in the Arm (1989)★
❑ ❑   2 - A Second Shot in the Dark (1990)
❑ ❑   3 - Bad Monday (1998)
❑ ❑   . . . .
❑ ❑   . . . .

ROSS, Annie [P]
Bel Carson

❑ ❑   1 - Moving Image (1995)
❑ ❑   2 - Shot in the Dark (1996)
❑ ❑   3 - Double Vision (1997)
❑ ❑   . . . .
❑ ❑   . . . .

ROSS, Kate
Julian Kestrel

❑ ❑   1 - Cut to the Quick (1993)
❑ ❑   2 - A Broken Vessel (1994)★
❑ ❑   3 - Whom the Gods Love (1995)
❑ ❑   4 - The Devil in Music (1997)★
❑ ❑   . . . .
❑ ❑   . . . .

ROTHENBERG, Rebecca
Claire Sharples

❑ ❑   1 - The Bulrush Murders (1991)☆☆
❑ ❑   2 - The Dandelion Murders (1994)
❑ ❑   3 - The Shy Tulip Murders (1996)
❑ ❑   . . . .
❑ ❑   . . . .

ROWE, Jennifer
Verity "Birdie" Birdwood

❑ ❑   1 - Murder by the Book (1989)
❑ ❑   2 - Grim Pickings (1991)
❑ ❑   ss - Death in Store [short stories] (1992)
❑ ❑   3 - The Makeover Murders (1993)

❏ ❏   4 - Stranglehold (1994)
❏ ❏   5 - Lamb to the Slaughter (1995)
❏ ❏   . . . .
❏ ❏   . . . .

ROWLAND, Laura Joh

new

Ichiro Sano

❏ ❏   1 - Shinju (1994)☆
❏ ❏   2 - Bundori (1996)
❏ ❏   3 - The Way of the Traitor (1997)
❏ ❏   4 - The Concubine's Tattoo (1998)
❏ ❏   . . . .
❏ ❏   . . . .

ROWLANDS, Betty

Melissa Craig

❏ ❏   1 - A Little Gentle Sleuthing (1990)
❏ ❏   2 - Finishing Touch (1993)
❏ ❏   3 - Over the Edge (1993)
❏ ❏   4 - Exhaustive Inquiries (1994)
❏ ❏   5 - Malice Poetic (1995)
❏ ❏   6 - Smiling at Death (1995)
❏ ❏   7 - Deadly Legacy (1996)
❏ ❏   8 - The Cherry Pickers (1997)
❏ ❏   . . . .
❏ ❏   . . . .

Sukey Reynolds

❏ ❏   1 - A Hive of Bees (1996)
❏ ❏   2 - An Inconsiderate Death (1997)
❏ ❏   3 - Death at Dearley Manor (1998)
❏ ❏   . . . .
❏ ❏   . . . .

ROZAN, S. J.

Lydia Chin & Bill Smith

❏ ❏   1 - China Trade (1994)
❏ ❏   2 - Concourse (1995)★
❏ ❏   3 - Mandarin Plaid (1996)
❏ ❏   4 - No Colder Place (1997)☆

❑ ❑   5 - A Bitter Feast (1998)
❑ ❑   6 - Stone Quarry (1999)
❑ ❑   . . . .
❑ ❑   . . . .

RUBINO, Jane

Cat Austen & Victor Cardenas

❑ ❑   1 - Death of a DJ (1996)
❑ ❑   2 - Fruitcake (1997)
❑ ❑   3 - Cheat the Devil (1998)
❑ ❑   . . . .
❑ ❑   . . . .

RURYK, Jean

Catherine Wilde

❑ ❑   1 - Chicken Little Was Right (1994)
❑ ❑   2 - Whatever Happened to Jennifer Steele? (1996)
❑ ❑   3 - Next Week Will Be Better (1998)
❑ ❑   . . . .
❑ ❑   . . . .

RUSHFORD, Patricia H.

Helen Bradley

❑ ❑   1 - Now I Lay Me Down to Sleep (1997)
❑ ❑   2 - Red Sky in Mourning (1997)
❑ ❑   3 - A Haunting Refrain (1998)
❑ ❑   . . . .
❑ ❑   . . . .

RUST, Megan Mallory

Taylor Morgan

❑ ❑   1 - Dead Stick (1998)
❑ ❑   2 - Redline (1999)
❑ ❑   3 - Coffin Corner (1999)
❑ ❑   4 - Graveyard Spiral (2000)
❑ ❑   . . . .
❑ ❑   . . . .

SALE, Medora

John Sanders & Harriet Jeffries

❑ ❑   1 - Murder on the Run (1986)★
❑ ❑   2 - Murder in Focus (1989)
❑ ❑   3 - Murder in a Good Cause (1990)
❑ ❑   4 - Sleep of the Innocent (1991)
❑ ❑   5 - Pursued by Shadows (1992)
❑ ❑   6 - Short Cut to Santa Fe (1994)
❑ ❑   . . . .
❑ ❑   . . . .

SALTER, Anna

Michael Stone

❑ ❑   1 - Shiny Water (1997)
❑ ❑   2 - Fault Lines (1998)
❑ ❑   . . . .
❑ ❑   . . . .

SANDSTROM, Eve K.

Nell Matthews & Mike Svenson

❑ ❑   1 - The Violence Beat (1997)
❑ ❑   2 - The Homicide Report (1998)
❑ ❑   . . . .
❑ ❑   . . . .

Sam & Nicky Titus

❑ ❑   1 - Death Down Home (1990)
❑ ❑   2 - The Devil down Home (1991)
❑ ❑   3 - The Down Home Heifer Heist (1993)
❑ ❑   . . . .
❑ ❑   . . . .

SANTINI, Rosemarie

Rick & Rosie Caesare Ramsey

❑ ❑   1 - A Swell Style of Murder (1986)
❑ ❑   2 - The Disenchanted Diva (1987)
❑ ❑   . . . .
❑ ❑   . . . .

SAUM, Karen

Brigid Donovan

❑ ❑   1 - Murder Is Relative (1990)
❑ ❑   2 - Murder Is Germane (1992)
❑ ❑   3 - Murder Is Material (1994)
❑ ❑   . . . .
❑ ❑   . . . .

SAWYER, Corinne Holt

Angela Benbow & Caledonia Wingate

❑ ❑   1 - The J. Alfred Prufrock Murders (1988)☆
❑ ❑   2 - Murder in Gray & White (1989)
❑ ❑   3 - Murder by Owl Light (1992)
❑ ❑   4 - The Peanut Butter Murders (1993)
❑ ❑   5 - Murder Has No Calories (1994)
❑ ❑   6 - Ho-Ho Homicide (1995)
❑ ❑   7 - The Geezer Factory Murders (1996)
❑ ❑   8 - Murder Ole (1997)
❑ ❑   . . . .
❑ ❑   . . . .

SCHIER, Norma

Kay Barth

❑ ❑   1 - Death on the Slopes (1978)
❑ ❑   2 - Murder by the Book (1979)
❑ ❑   3 - Death Goes Skiing (1979)
❑ ❑   4 - Demon at the Opera (1980)
❑ ❑   . . . .
❑ ❑   . . . .

SCHMIDT, Carol

Laney Samms

❑ ❑   1 - Silverlake Heat (1993)
❑ ❑   2 - Sweet Cherry Wine (1994)
❑ ❑   3 - Cabin Fever (1994)
❑ ❑   . . . .
❑ ❑   . . . .

SCHUMACHER, Aileen

Tory Travers

❏ ❏ 1 - Engineered for Murder (1996)
❏ ❏ 2 - Framework for Death (1998)
❏ ❏ 3 - Affirmative Reaction (1999)
❏ ❏ . . . .
❏ ❏ . . . .

SCOPPETTONE, Sandra

Lauren Laurano

❏ ❏ 1 - Everything You Have Is Mine (1991)
❏ ❏ 2 - I'll Be Leaving You Always (1993)
❏ ❏ 3 - My Sweet Untraceable You (1994)
❏ ❏ 4 - Let's Face the Music and Die (1996)
❏ ❏ 5 - Gonna Take a Homicidal Journey (1998)
❏ ❏ . . . .
❏ ❏ . . . .

SCOTT, Barbara A.

Brad Rollins et al

❏ ❏ 1 - Always in a Foreign Land (1993)
❏ ❏ 2 - Caught in the Web (1996)
❏ ❏ 3 - Pay Out & Pay Back (1999)
❏ ❏ . . . .
❏ ❏ . . . .

SCOTTOLINE, Lisa

Rosato & Associates

❏ ❏ 1 - Everywhere That Mary Went
           [Mary DiNunzio] (1993)☆
❏ ❏ 2 - Final Appeal [Grace Rossi] (1994)★
❏ ❏ 3 - Running From the Law [Rita Morrone] (1995)
❏ ❏ 4 - Legal Tender [Bennie Rosato] (1996)
❏ ❏ 5 - Rough Justice [Marta Richter] (1997)
❏ ❏ 6 - Mistaken Identity [Rosato et al] (1999)
❏ ❏ . . . .
❏ ❏ . . . .

SEDLEY, Kate [P]
Roger the Chapman
❑ ❑   1 - Death and the Chapman (1991)
❑ ❑   2 - The Plymouth Cloak (1992)
❑ ❑   3 - The Weaver's Tale (1993)
❑ ❑   - APA-The Hanged Man
❑ ❑   4 - The Holy Innocents (1994)
❑ ❑   5 - Eve of St. Hyacinth (1996)
❑ ❑   6 - The Wicked Winter (1996)
❑ ❑   7 - The Brothers of Glastonbury (1997)
❑ ❑   . . . .
❑ ❑   . . . .

SHABER, Sarah R.
Simon Shaw
❑ ❑   1 - Simon Said (1997)★
❑ ❑   2 - Snipe Hunt (1999)
❑ ❑   . . . .
❑ ❑   . . . .

SHAFFER, Louise
Angie DaVito
❑ ❑   1 - All My Suspects (1994)
❑ ❑   2 - Talked to Death (1995)
❑ ❑   . . . .
❑ ❑   . . . .

SHAH, Diane K.
Paris Chandler
❑ ❑   1 - As Crime Goes By (1990)
❑ ❑   2 - Dying Cheek to Cheek (1992)
❑ ❑   . . . .
❑ ❑   . . . .

SHANKMAN, Sarah
Samantha Adams
❑ ❑   1 - First Kill All the Lawyers (1988)
❑ ❑   2 - Then Hang All the Liars (1989)
❑ ❑   3 - Now Let's Talk of Graves (1990)

❑ ❑ 4 - She Walks in Beauty (1991)
❑ ❑ 5 - The King Is Dead (1992)
❑ ❑ 6 - He Was Her Man (1993)
❑ ❑ 7 - Digging Up Momma (1998)
❑ ❑   . . . .
❑ ❑   . . . .

SHAW, P. B. [P]
Abe Rainfinch
❑ ❑ 1 - The Seraphim Kill (1994)
❑ ❑ 2 - The Water Cannibals (1996)
❑ ❑   . . . .
❑ ❑   . . . .

SHELTON, Connie
Charlie Parker
❑ ❑ 1 - Deadly Gamble (1995)
❑ ❑ 2 - Vacations Can Be Murder (1995)
❑ ❑ 3 - Partnerships Can Kill (1997)
❑ ❑ 4 - Small Towns Can Be Murder (1998)
❑ ❑   . . . .
❑ ❑   . . . .

SHEPHERD, Stella
Richard Montgomery
❑ ❑ 1 - Black Justice (1989)
❑ ❑ 2 - Murderous Remedy (1990)
❑ ❑ 3 - Thinner Than Blood (1992)
❑ ❑ 4 - A Lethal Fixation (1993)
❑ ❑ 5 - Nurse Dawes Is Dead (1994)
❑ ❑ 6 - Something in the Cellar (1995)
❑ ❑ 7 - Embers of Death (1996)
❑ ❑   . . . .
❑ ❑   . . . .

SHERIDAN, Juanita
Lily Wu & Janice Cameron
- ❏ ❏ 1 - The Chinese Chop (1949)
- ❏ ❏ 2 - The Kahuna Killer (1951)
- ❏ ❏ 3 - The Mamo Murders (1952)
- ❏ ❏   - Brit.-While the Coffin Waited
- ❏ ❏ 4 - The Waikiki Widow (1953)
- ❏ ❏ . . . .
- ❏ ❏ . . . .

SHERMAN, Beth
Anne Hardaway
- ❏ ❏ 1 - Dead Man's Float (1998)
- ❏ ❏ 2 - Acting Is Murder (1999)
- ❏ ❏ . . . .
- ❏ ❏ . . . .

SHONE, Anna
Ulysses Finnegan Donaghue
- ❏ ❏ 1 - Mr. Donaghue Investigates (1995)
- ❏ ❏ 2 - Secrets in Stones (1996)
- ❏ ❏ . . . .
- ❏ ❏ . . . .

SHORT, Sharon Gwyn
Patricia Delaney
- ❏ ❏ 1 - Angel's Bidding (1994)
- ❏ ❏ 2 - Past Pretense (1994)
- ❏ ❏ 3 - The Death We Share (1995)
- ❏ ❏ . . . .
- ❏ ❏ . . . .

SIBLEY, Celestine
Kate Kincaid Mulcay
- ❏ ❏ 1 - The Malignant Heart (1958)
- ❏ ❏ 2 - Ah, Sweet Mystery (1991)
- ❏ ❏ 3 - Straight as an Arrow (1992)

❏ ❏   4 - Dire Happenings at Scratch Ankle (1993)
❏ ❏   5 - A Plague of Kinfolks (1995)
❏ ❏   6 - Spider in the Sink (1997)
❏ ❏   . . . .
❏ ❏   . . . .

SILVA, Linda Kay

Delta Stevens

❏ ❏   1 - Taken by Storm (1991)
❏ ❏   2 - Storm Shelter (1993)
❏ ❏   3 - Weathering the Storm (1994)
❏ ❏   4 - Storm Front (1995)
❏ ❏   . . . .
❏ ❏   . . . .

SIMONSON, Sheila

Lark Dailey

❏ ❏   1 - Larkspur (1990)
❏ ❏   2 - Skylark (1992)
❏ ❏   3 - Mudlark (1993)
❏ ❏   4 - Meadowlark (1996)
❏ ❏   5 - Malarkey (1997)
❏ ❏   . . . .
❏ ❏   . . . .

SIMPSON, Dorothy

Luke Thanet

❏ ❏   1 - The Night She Died (1981)
❏ ❏   2 - Six Feet Under (1982)
❏ ❏   3 - Puppet for a Corpse (1983)
❏ ❏   4 - Close Her Eyes (1984)
❏ ❏   5 - Last Seen Alive (1985)★
❏ ❏   6 - Dead on Arrival (1986)
❏ ❏   7 - Element of Doubt (1987)
❏ ❏   8 - Suspicious Death (1988)
❏ ❏   9 - Dead by Morning (1989)
❏ ❏ 10 - Doomed To Die (1991)
❏ ❏ 11 - Wake Her Dead (1992)

❏ ❏ 12 - No Laughing Matter (1993)
❏ ❏ 13 - A Day for Dying (1995)
❏ ❏ 14 - Once Too Often (1997)
❏ ❏ . . . .
❏ ❏ . . . .

SIMS, L. V.
Dixie T. Struthers
❏ ❏ 1 - Murder Is Only Skin Deep (1987)
❏ ❏ 2 - Death Is a Family Affair (1987)
❏ ❏ 3 - To Sleep, Perchance to Kill (1988)
❏ ❏ . . . .
❏ ❏ . . . .

SINGER, Shelley
Barrett Lake
❏ ❏ 1 - Following Jane (1993)
❏ ❏ 2 - Picture of David (1993)
❏ ❏ 3 - Searching for Sara (1994)
❏ ❏ 4 - Interview With Mattie (1995)☆
❏ ❏ . . . .
❏ ❏ . . . .

Jake Samson & Rosie Vicente
❏ ❏ 1 - Samson's Deal (1983)
❏ ❏ 2 - Free Draw (1984)
❏ ❏ 3 - Full House (1986)
❏ ❏ 4 - Spit in the Ocean (1987)
❏ ❏ 5 - Suicide King (1988)
❏ ❏ . . . .
❏ ❏ . . . .

SJÖWALL, Maj & Per Wahlöö
Martin Beck
❏ ❏ 1 - Roseanna (1965)
❏ ❏ 2 - The Man Who Went Up in Smoke (1966)
❏ ❏ 3 - The Man on the Balcony (1967)
❏ ❏ 4 - The Laughing Policeman (1968)★
❏ ❏ 5 - The Fire Engine That Disappeared (1969)
❏ ❏ 6 - Murder at the Savoy (1970)

❏ ❏   7 - The Abominable Man (1971)
❏ ❏   8 - The Locked Room (1972)
❏ ❏   9 - Cop Killer (1974)
❏ ❏ 10 - The Terrorists (1975)
❏ ❏   . . . .
❏ ❏   . . . .

SKOM, Edith
Elizabeth Austin
❏ ❏   1 - The Mark Twain Murders (1989)☆☆
❏ ❏   2 - The George Eliot Murders (1995)
❏ ❏   3 - The Charles Dickens Murders (1998)
❏ ❏   . . . .
❏ ❏   . . . .

SLEEM, Patty
Maggie Dillitz
❏ ❏   1 - Back in Time (1997)
❏ ❏   2 - Fall From Grace (1999)
❏ ❏   . . . .
❏ ❏   . . . .

SLOVO, Gillian
Kate Baeier
❏ ❏   1 - Morbid Symptoms (1984)
❏ ❏   2 - Death Comes Staccato (1987)
❏ ❏   3 - Death by Analysis (1988)
❏ ❏   4 - Catnap (1994)
❏ ❏   5 - Close Call (1995)
❏ ❏   . . . .
❏ ❏   . . . .

SMITH, Alison
Judd Springfield
❏ ❏   1 - Someone Else's Grave (1984)☆
❏ ❏   2 - Rising (1987)
❏ ❏   . . . .
❏ ❏   . . . .

SMITH, Barbara Burnett

Jolie Wyatt

- ❏ ❏ 1 - Writers of the Purple Sage (1994)☆
- ❏ ❏ 2 - Dust Devils of the Purple Sage (1995)
- ❏ ❏ 3 - Celebration in Purple Sage (1996)
- ❏ ❏ 4 - Mistletoe From Purple Sage (1997)
- ❏ ❏ ....
- ❏ ❏ ....

SMITH, Cynthia

Emma Rhodes

- ❏ ❏ 1 - Noblesse Oblige (1996)
- ❏ ❏ 2 - Impolite Society (1997)
- ❏ ❏ 3 - Misleading Ladies (1997)
- ❏ ❏ 4 - Silver and Guilt (1998)
- ❏ ❏ ....
- ❏ ❏ ....

SMITH, Evelyn E.

Susan Melville

- ❏ ❏ 1 - Miss Melville Regrets (1986)
- ❏ ❏ 2 - Miss Melville Returns (1987)
- ❏ ❏ 3 - Miss Melville's Revenge (1989)
- ❏ ❏ 4 - Miss Melville Rides a Tiger (1991)
- ❏ ❏ ....
- ❏ ❏ ....

SMITH, J. C. S. [P]

Quentin Jacoby

- ❏ ❏ 1 - Jacoby's First Case (1980)
- ❏ ❏ 2 - Nightcap (1984)
- ❏ ❏ ....
- ❏ ❏ ....

SMITH, Janet L.

Annie MacPherson

- ❏ ❏   1 - Sea of Troubles (1990)☆
- ❏ ❏   2 - Practice to Deceive (1992)
- ❏ ❏   3 - A Vintage Murder (1994)
- ❏ ❏   . . . .
- ❏ ❏   . . . .

SMITH, Joan

Loretta Lawson

- ❏ ❏   1 - A Masculine Ending (1987)
- ❏ ❏   2 - Why Aren't They Screaming? (1988)
- ❏ ❏   3 - Don't Leave Me This Way (1990)
- ❏ ❏   4 - What Men Say (1993)
- ❏ ❏   5 - Full Stop (1995)
- ❏ ❏   . . . .
- ❏ ❏   . . . .

SMITH, Joan G.

Cassie Newton

- ❏ ❏   1 - Capriccio (1989)
- ❏ ❏   2 - A Brush With Death (1990)
- ❏ ❏   . . . .
- ❏ ❏   . . . .

SMITH, Julie

Paul MacDonald

- ❏ ❏   1 - True-Life Adventure (1985)
- ❏ ❏   2 - Huckleberry Fiend (1987)
- ❏ ❏   . . . .
- ❏ ❏   . . . .

Rebecca Schwartz

- ❏ ❏   1 - Death Turns a Trick (1982)
- ❏ ❏   2 - The Sourdough Wars (1984)
- ❏ ❏   3 - Tourist Trap (1986)
- ❏ ❏   4 - Dead in the Water (1991)
- ❏ ❏   5 - Other People's Skeletons (1993)
- ❏ ❏   . . . .
- ❏ ❏   . . . .

Skip Langdon
❏ ❏ 1 - New Orleans Mourning (1990)★☆
❏ ❏ 2 - The Axeman's Jazz (1991)
❏ ❏ 3 - Jazz Funeral (1993)
❏ ❏ 4 - New Orleans Beat (1994)
❏ ❏ 5 - House of Blues (1995)
❏ ❏ 6 - The Kindness of Strangers (1996)
❏ ❏ 7 - Crescent City Kill (1997)
❏ ❏ 8 - 82 Desire (1998)
❏ ❏ ....
❏ ❏ ....

SMITH, Sarah
Alexander von Riesden
❏ ❏ 1 - The Vanished Child [Boston] (1994)
❏ ❏ 2 - The Knowledge of Water [Paris] (1996)
❏ ❏ ....
❏ ❏ ....

SMITH-LEVIN, Judith
Starletta DuVall
❏ ❏ 1 - Do Not Go Gently (1996)
❏ ❏ 2 - The Hoodoo Man (1997)
❏ ❏ 3 - Green Money (1998)
❏ ❏ ....
❏ ❏ ....

SONGER, C. J.
Meg Gillis
❏ ❏ 1 - Bait (1998)
❏ ❏ 2 - Hook (1999)
❏ ❏ ....
❏ ❏ ....

SPEART, Jessica
Rachel Porter
❏ ❏ 1 - Gator Aide (1997)
❏ ❏ 2 - Tortoise Soup (1998)
❏ ❏ 3 - Bird Brained (1999)
❏ ❏ ....
❏ ❏ ....

SPRAGUE, Gretchen
Martha Patterson
- ❏ ❏ 1 - Death in Good Company (1997)
- ❏ ❏ 2 - Maquette for Murder (1999)
- ❏ ❏ . . . .
- ❏ ❏ . . . .

SPRING, Michelle
Laura Principal
- ❏ ❏ 1 - Every Breath You Take (1994)☆
- ❏ ❏ 2 - Running for Shelter (1995)
- ❏ ❏ 3 - Standing in the Shadows (1998)
- ❏ ❏ 4 - Nights in White Satin (1999)
- ❏ ❏ . . . .
- ❏ ❏ . . . .

SPRINKLE, Patricia H.
MacLaren Yarbrough
- ❏ ❏ 1 - When Did We Lose Harriet? (1997)
- ❏ ❏ 2 - But Why Shoot the Magistrate? (1998)
- ❏ ❏ . . . .
- ❏ ❏ . . . .

Sheila Travis
- ❏ ❏ 1 - Murder at Markham (1988)
- ❏ ❏ 2 - Murder in the Charleston Manner (1990)
- ❏ ❏ 3 - Murder on Peachtree Street (1991)
- ❏ ❏ 4 - Somebody's Dead in Snellville (1992)
- ❏ ❏ 5 - Death of a Dunwoody Matron (1993)
- ❏ ❏ 6 - A Mystery Bred in Buckhead (1994)
- ❏ ❏ 7 - Deadly Secrets on the St. Johns (1995)
- ❏ ❏ . . . .
- ❏ ❏ . . . .

SQUIRE, Elizabeth Daniels
Peaches Dann
- ❏ ❏ 1 - Who Killed What's-Her-Name? (1994)
- ❏ ❏ 2 - Remember the Alibi (1994)
- ❏ ❏ 3 - Memory Can Be Murder (1995)
- ❏ ❏ 4 - Whose Death Is It Anyway? (1997)

❑ ❑   5 - Is There a Dead Man in the House? (1998)
❑ ❑   6 - Where There's a Will (1999)
❑ ❑   . . . .
❑ ❑   . . . .

STABENOW, Dana

Kate Shugak

❑ ❑   1 - A Cold Day for Murder (1992)★
❑ ❑   2 - A Fatal Thaw (1993)
❑ ❑   3 - Dead in the Water (1993)
❑ ❑   4 - A Cold-Blooded Business (1994)
❑ ❑   5 - Play With Fire (1995)
❑ ❑   6 - Blood Will Tell (1996)
❑ ❑   7 - Breakup (1997)
❑ ❑   8 - Killing Grounds (1998)
❑ ❑   9 - Hunter's Moon (1999)
❑ ❑ 10 - Tailspin (2000)
❑ ❑   . . . .
❑ ❑   . . . .

Liam Campbell & Wyanet Chouinard

❑ ❑   1 - Fire and Ice (1998)
❑ ❑   2 - So Sure of Death (1999)
❑ ❑   3 - Nothing Gold Can Say (2000)
❑ ❑   . . . .
❑ ❑   . . . .

STACEY, Susannah [P]

Robert Bone

❑ ❑   1 - Goodbye Nanny Gray (1987)☆
❑ ❑   2 - A Knife at the Opera (1988)
❑ ❑   3 - Body of Opinion (1988)
❑ ❑   4 - Grave Responsibility (1990)
❑ ❑   5 - The Late Lady (1992)
❑ ❑   6 - Bone Idle (1993)
❑ ❑   7 - Dead Serious (1995)
❑ ❑   . . . .
❑ ❑   . . . .

STAINCLIFFE, Cath
Sal Kilkenny
❏ ❏   1 - Looking for Trouble (1994)☆
❏ ❏   2 - Go Not Gently (1997)
❏ ❏   3 - Dead Wrong (1998)
❏ ❏   . . . .
❏ ❏   . . . .

STALLWOOD, Veronica
Kate Ivory
❏ ❏   1 - Death and the Oxford Box (1993)
❏ ❏   2 - Oxford Exit (1995)
❏ ❏   3 - Oxford Mourning (1996)
❏ ❏   4 - Oxford Fall (1996)
❏ ❏   5 - Oxford Knot (1998)
❏ ❏   . . . .
❏ ❏   . . . .

STAR, Nancy
May Morrison
❏ ❏   1 - Up Next (1998)
❏ ❏   2 - Now This (1999)
❏ ❏   . . . .
❏ ❏   . . . .

STEIN, Triss
Kay Engles
❏ ❏   1 - Murder at the Class Reunion (1993)
❏ ❏   2 - Digging Up Death (1998)
❏ ❏   . . . .
❏ ❏   . . . .

STEINBERG, Janice
Margo Simon
❏ ❏   1 - Death of a Postmodernist (1995)
❏ ❏   2 - Death Crosses the Border (1995)
❏ ❏   3 - Death-Fires Dance (1996)

❏ ❏   4 - The Dead Man and the Sea (1997)
❏ ❏   5 - Death in a City of Mystics (1998)
❏ ❏   . . . .
❏ ❏   . . . .

STEINER, Susan
Alex Winter

❏ ❏   1 - Murder on Her Mind (1991)
❏ ❏   2 - Library: No Murder Aloud (1993)
❏ ❏   . . . .
❏ ❏   . . . .

STEVENS, Serita
Fanny Zindel

❏ ❏   1 - Red Sea, Dead Sea (1991)
❏ ❏   2 - Bagels for Tea (1993)
❏ ❏   . . . .
❏ ❏   . . . .

STRUTHERS, Betsy
Rosalie Cairns

❏ ❏   1 - Found: A Body (1992)
❏ ❏   2 - Grave Deeds (1994)
❏ ❏   3 - A Studied Death (1995)
❏ ❏   . . . .
❏ ❏   . . . .

STUBBS, Jean
John Joseph Lintott

❏ ❏   1 - Dear Laura (1973)☆
❏ ❏   2 - The Painted Face (1974)
❏ ❏   3 - The Golden Crucible (1976)
❏ ❏   . . . .
❏ ❏   . . . .

STUYCK, Karen Hanson

Liz James

❑ ❑   1 - Cry for Help (1995)
❑ ❑   2 - Held Accountable (1996)
❑ ❑   3 - Lethal Lessons (1997)
❑ ❑   . . . .
❑ ❑   . . . .

SUCHER, Dorothy

Sabina Swift

❑ ❑   1 - Dead Men Don't Give Seminars (1988)☆
❑ ❑   2 - Dead Men Don't Marry (1989)
❑ ❑   . . . .
❑ ❑   . . . .

SULLIVAN, Winona

Cecile Buddenbrooks

❑ ❑   1 - A Sudden Death at the Norfolk Café (1993)★
❑ ❑   2 - Dead South (1996)
❑ ❑   3 - Death's a Beach (1998)
❑ ❑   . . . .
❑ ❑   . . . .

SUMNER, Penny

Victoria Cross

❑ ❑   1 - The End of April (1992)
❑ ❑   2 - Crosswords (1995)
❑ ❑   . . . .
❑ ❑   . . . .

SZYMANSKI, Therese

Brett Higgins

❑ ❑   1 - When the Dancing Stops (1997)
❑ ❑   2 - When the Dead Speak (1998)
❑ ❑   3 - When Some Body Disappears (1999)
❑ ❑   4 - When First We Practice (1999)
❑ ❑   . . . .
❑ ❑   . . . .

TAN, Maureen
Jane Nichols
- ❏ ❏ 1 - aka Jane (1997)
- ❏ ❏ 2 - Run, Jane, Run (1999)
- ❏ ❏ . . . .
- ❏ ❏ . . . .

TAYLOR, Alison G. [P]
Michael Mckenna
- ❏ ❏ 1 - Simeon's Bride (1995)
- ❏ ❏ 2 - In Guilty Night (1996)
- ❏ ❏ 3 - House of Women (1998)
- ❏ ❏ . . . .
- ❏ ❏ . . . .

TAYLOR, Elizabeth Atwood
Maggie Elliott
- ❏ ❏ 1 - The Cable Car Murder (1981)
- ❏ ❏ 2 - Murder at Vassar (1987)
- ❏ ❏ 3 - The Northwest Murders (1992)
- ❏ ❏ . . . .
- ❏ ❏ . . . .

TAYLOR, Jean
Maggie Garrett
- ❏ ❏ 1 - We Know Where You Live (1995)
- ❏ ❏ 2 - The Last of Her Lies (1996)
- ❏ ❏ . . . .
- ❏ ❏ . . . .

TAYLOR, Kathleen
Tory Bauer
- ❏ ❏ 1 - The Missionary Position (1995)
- ❏ ❏   - APA-Funeral Food (1997)
- ❏ ❏ 2 - Sex and Salmonella (1996)
- ❏ ❏ 3 - The Hotel South Dakota (1997)
- ❏ ❏ 4 - Mourning Shift (1998)
- ❏ ❏ . . . .
- ❏ ❏ . . . .

TAYLOR, L. A.
J. J. Jamison
❑ ❑   1 - Only Half a Hoax (1984)
❑ ❑   2 - Deadly Objectives (1985)
❑ ❑   3 - Shed Light on Death (1985)
❑ ❑   4 - A Murder Waiting to Happen (1989)
❑ ❑   . . . .
❑ ❑   . . . .

TELL, Dorothy
Poppy Dillworth
❑ ❑   1 - Murder at Red Rook Ranch (1990)
❑ ❑   2 - Wilderness Trek (1990)
❑ ❑   3 - The Hallelujah Murders (1991)
❑ ❑   . . . .
❑ ❑   . . . .

TEMPLE, Lou Jane
Heaven Lee
❑ ❑   1 - Death by Rhubarb (1996)
❑ ❑   2 - Revenge of the Barbecue Queens (1997)
❑ ❑   3 - A Stiff Risotto (1997)
❑ ❑   4 - Bread on Arrival (1998)
❑ ❑   . . . .
❑ ❑   . . . .

TESLER, Nancy
Carrie Carlin
❑ ❑   1 - Pink Balloons and Other Deadly Things (1997)
❑ ❑   2 - Sharks, Jellyfish and Other Deadly Things (1998)
❑ ❑   3 - Sticks & Stones and Other Deadly Things (1999)
❑ ❑   . . . .
❑ ❑   . . . .

THOMAS-GRAHAM, Pamela
Nikki Chase
❑ ❑   1 - A Darker Shade of Crimson [Harvard] (1998)
❑ ❑   2 - Blue Blood [Yale] (1999)
❑ ❑   . . . .
❑ ❑   . . . .

THOMSON, June

Inspector Finch

- ❏ ❏   1 - Not One of Us (1971)
- ❏ ❏   2 - Death Cap (1973)
- ❏ ❏   3 - The Long Revenge (1974)
- ❏ ❏   4 - Case Closed (1977)
- ❏ ❏   5 - A Question of Identity (1977)
- ❏ ❏   6 - Deadly Relations (1979)
- ❏ ❏   - U.S.-The Habit of Loving
- ❏ ❏   7 - Alibi in Time (1980)
- ❏ ❏   8 - Shadow of a Doubt (1981)
- ❏ ❏   9 - To Make a Killing (1982)
- ❏ ❏   - U.S.-Portrait of Lilith
- ❏ ❏ 10 - Sound Evidence (1984)
- ❏ ❏ 11 - A Dying Fall (1985)
- ❏ ❏ 12 - The Dark Stream (1986)
- ❏ ❏ 13 - No Flowers by Request (1987)
- ❏ ❏ 14 - Rosemary for Remembrance (1988)
- ❏ ❏ 15 - The Spoils of Time (1989)
- ❏ ❏ 16 - Past Reckoning (1990)
- ❏ ❏ 17 - Foul Play (1991)
- ❏ ❏ 18 - Burden of Innocence (1996)
- ❏ ❏ . . . .
- ❏ ❏ . . . .

THRASHER, L. L. [P]

Lizbet Lange

- ❏ ❏   1 - Charlie's Bones (1997)
- ❏ ❏ . . . .
- ❏ ❏ . . . .

Zachariah Smith

- ❏ ❏   1 - Cat's-Paw, Inc. (1992)
- ❏ ❏   2 - Dogsbody, Inc. (1998)
- ❏ ❏ . . . .
- ❏ ❏ . . . .

THURLO, Aimee & David

Ella Clah

- ❏ ❏   1 - Blackening Song (1995)
- ❏ ❏   2 - Death Walker (1996)

❏ ❏   3 - Bad Medicine (1997)
❏ ❏   4 - Enemy Way (1998)
❏ ❏   5 - Shooting Chant (1999)
❏ ❏   . . . .
❏ ❏   . . . .

TISHY, Cecelia

Kate Banning

❏ ❏   1 - Jealous Heart (1997)
❏ ❏   2 - Cryin' Time (1998)
❏ ❏   . . . .
❏ ❏   . . . .

TODD, Marilyn

Claudia Seferius

❏ ❏   1 - I, Claudia (1995)
❏ ❏   2 - Virgin Territory (1996)
❏ ❏   3 - Man Eater (1997)
❏ ❏   4 - Wolf Whistle (1998)
❏ ❏   . . . .
❏ ❏   . . . .

TONE, Teona

Kyra Keaton

❏ ❏   1 - Lady on the Line (1983)
❏ ❏   2 - Full Cry (1985)
❏ ❏   . . . .
❏ ❏   . . . .

TRAVIS, Elizabeth

Ben & Carrie Porter

❏ ❏   1 - Under the Influence (1989)
❏ ❏   2 - Finders Keepers (1990)
❏ ❏   . . . .
❏ ❏   . . . .

TROCHECK, Kathy Hogan

Callahan Garrity

❏ ❏   1 - Every Crooked Nanny (1992)☆☆
❏ ❏   2 - To Live and Die in Dixie (1993)☆☆

❏ ❏ 3 - Homemade Sin (1994)
❏ ❏ 4 - Happy Never After (1995)
❏ ❏ 5 - Heart Trouble (1996)
❏ ❏ 6 - Strange Brew (1997)
❏ ❏ 7 - Midnight Clear (1998)
❏ ❏ . . . .
❏ ❏ . . . .

Truman Kicklighter

❏ ❏ 1 - Lickety Split (1996)
❏ ❏ 2 - Crash Course (1997)
❏ ❏ . . . .
❏ ❏ . . . .

TRUMAN, Margaret
Mackenzie Smith & Annabel Reed

❏ ❏ 1 - Murder at the Kennedy Center (1989)
❏ ❏ 2 - Murder at the National Cathedral (1990)
❏ ❏ 3 - Murder at the Pentagon (1992)
❏ ❏ 4 - Murder on the Potomac (1994)
❏ ❏ 5 - Murder at the National Gallery (1996)
❏ ❏ 6 - Murder in the House (1997)
❏ ❏ 7 - Murder at the Watergate (1998)
❏ ❏ . . . .
❏ ❏ . . . .

TUCKER, Kerry
Libby Kincaid

❏ ❏ 1 - Still Waters (1991)
❏ ❏ 2 - Cold Feet (1992)
❏ ❏ 3 - Death Echo (1993)
❏ ❏ 4 - Drift Away (1994)
❏ ❏ . . . .
❏ ❏ . . . .

TYRE, Peg
Kate Murray

❏ ❏ 1 - Strangers in the Night (1994)
❏ ❏ 2 - In the Midnight Hour (1995)
❏ ❏ . . . .
❏ ❏ . . . .

UHNAK, Dorothy

Christine Opara

❑ ❑   1 - The Bait (1968)★
❑ ❑   2 - The Witness (1969)
❑ ❑   3 - The Ledger (1970)★
❑ ❑   . . . .
❑ ❑   . . . .

VALENTINE, Deborah
Katharine Craig & Kevin Bryce
- ❑ ❑ 1 - Unorthodox Methods (1989)
- ❑ ❑ 2 - A Collector of Photographs (1989)☆☆☆
- ❑ ❑ 3 - Fine Distinctions (1991)☆
- ❑ ❑ . . . .
- ❑ ❑ . . . .

VAN GIESON, Judith
Neil Hamel
- ❑ ❑ 1 - North of the Border (1988)
- ❑ ❑ 2 - Raptor (1990)
- ❑ ❑ 3 - The Other Side of Death (1991)
- ❑ ❑ 4 - The Wolf Path (1992)
- ❑ ❑ 5 - The Lies That Bind (1993)☆
- ❑ ❑ 6 - Parrot Blues (1995)
- ❑ ❑ 7 - Hotshots (1996)
- ❑ ❑ 8 - Ditch Rider (1998)
- ❑ ❑ . . . .
- ❑ ❑ . . . .

VAN HOOK, Beverly
Liza & Dutch Randolph
- ❑ ❑ 1 - Fiction, Fact, & Murder (1995)
- ❑ ❑ 2 - Juliet's Ghost (1999)
- ❑ ❑ . . . .
- ❑ ❑ . . . .

VIETS, Elaine
Francesca Vierling
- ❑ ❑ 1 - Backstab (1997)
- ❑ ❑ 2 - Rubout (1998)
- ❑ ❑ 3 - The Pink Flamingo Murders (1999)
- ❑ ❑ 4 - Home Wrecker (2000)
- ❑ ❑ . . . .
- ❑ ❑ . . . .

WAKEFIELD, Hannah [P]
Dee Street
- ❏ ❏ 1 - The Price You Pay (1987)
- ❏ ❏ 2 - A February Mourning (1990)
- ❏ ❏   - U.S.-A Woman's Own Mystery
- ❏ ❏ 3 - Cruel April (1997)
- ❏ ❏ . . . .
- ❏ ❏ . . . .

WALKER, Mary Willis
Kate Driscoll
- ❏ ❏ 1 - Zero at the Bone (1991)★★☆
- ❏ ❏ . . . .
- ❏ ❏ . . . .

Mollie Cates
- ❏ ❏ 1 - The Red Scream (1994)★☆
- ❏ ❏ 2 - Under the Beetle's Cellar (1995)★★★
- ❏ ❏ 3 - All the Dead Lie Down (1998)
- ❏ ❏ . . . .
- ❏ ❏ . . . .

WALLACE, Marilyn
Jay Goldstein & Carlos Cruz
- ❏ ❏ 1 - A Case of Loyalties (1986)★
- ❏ ❏ 2 - Primary Target (1988)☆
- ❏ ❏ 3 - A Single Stone (1991)☆
- ❏ ❏ . . . .
- ❏ ❏ . . . .

Theresa Gallagher
- ❏ ❏ 1 - Current Danger (1998)
- ❏ ❏ . . . .
- ❏ ❏ . . . .

WALLACE, Patricia
Sydney Bryant
❑ ❑   1 - Small Favors (1988)
❑ ❑   2 - Deadly Grounds (1989)
❑ ❑   3 - Blood Lies (1991)
❑ ❑   4 - Deadly Devotion (1994)☆
❑ ❑   . . . .
❑ ❑   . . . .

WALLINGFORD, Lee
Ginny Trask & Frank Carver
❑ ❑   1 - Cold Tracks (1991)
❑ ❑   2 - Clear Cut Murder (1993)
❑ ❑   . . . .
❑ ❑   . . . .

WALTCH, Lilla M.
Lisa Davis
❑ ❑   1 - The Third Victim (1987)
❑ ❑   2 - Fearful Symmetry (1988)
❑ ❑   . . . .
❑ ❑   . . . .

WARMBOLD, Jean
Sarah Calloway
❑ ❑   1 - June Mail (1986)
❑ ❑   2 - The White Hand (1988)
❑ ❑   3 - The Third Way (1989)
❑ ❑   . . . .
❑ ❑   . . . .

WARNER, Mignon
Edwina Charles
❑ ❑   1 - A Medium for Murder (1976)
❑ ❑   - Brit.-A Nice Way To Die
❑ ❑   2 - The Tarot Murders (1978)
❑ ❑   3 - Death in Time (1980)
❑ ❑   4 - The Girl Who Was Clairvoyant (1982)

❏ ❏   5 - Devil's Knell (1983)
❏ ❏   6 - Illusion (1984)
❏ ❏   7 - Speak No Evil (1985)
❏ ❏   . . . .
❏ ❏   . . . .

WARNER, Penny

Connor Westphal

❏ ❏   1 - Dead Body Language (1997)☆
❏ ❏   2 - Sign of Foul Play (1998)
❏ ❏   3 - Right to Remain Silent (1999)
❏ ❏   . . . .
❏ ❏   . . . .

WATERHOUSE, Jane

Garner Quin

❏ ❏   1 - Graven Images (1995)
❏ ❏   2 - Shadow Walk (1997)
❏ ❏   3 - Dead Letter (1998)
❏ ❏   . . . .
❏ ❏   . . . .

WATSON, Clarissa

Persis Willum

❏ ❏   1 - The Fourth Stage of Gainsborough Brown
                (1977)
❏ ❏   2 - The Bishop in the Back Seat (1980)
❏ ❏   3 - Runaway (1985)
❏ ❏   4 - Last Plane From Nice (1988)
❏ ❏   5 - Somebody Killed the Messenger (1988)
❏ ❏   . . . .
❏ ❏   . . . .

WEBB, Martha G. [P]

Tommy Inman

❏ ❏   1 - A White Male Running (1985)
❏ ❏   2 - Even Cops' Daughters (1986)
❏ ❏   . . . .
❏ ❏   . . . .

WEBER, Janice

Leslie Frost

- ❏ ❏   1 - Frost the Fiddler (1992)
- ❏ ❏   2 - Hot Ticket (1998)
- ❏ ❏   . . . .
- ❏ ❏   . . . .

WEIR, Charlene

Susan Wren

- ❏ ❏   1 - The Winter Widow (1992)★★☆
- ❏ ❏   2 - Consider the Crows (1993)☆
- ❏ ❏   3 - Family Practice (1995)
- ❏ ❏   4 - Lethal Promise (1997)
- ❏ ❏   5 - Murder Takes Two (1998)
- ❏ ❏   . . . .
- ❏ ❏   . . . .

WELCH, Pat

Helen Black

- ❏ ❏   1 - Murder by the Book (1990)
- ❏ ❏   2 - Still Waters (1992)
- ❏ ❏   3 - A Proper Burial (1993)
- ❏ ❏   4 - Open House (1995)
- ❏ ❏   5 - Smoke and Mirrors (1996)
- ❏ ❏   6 - Fallen From Grace (1998)
- ❏ ❏   . . . .
- ❏ ❏   . . . .

WELLS, Tobias [P]

Knute Severson

- ❏ ❏   1 - A Matter of Love and Death (1966)
- ❏ ❏   2 - Dead by the Light of the Moon (1967)
- ❏ ❏   3 - What Should You Know of Dying? (1967)
- ❏ ❏   4 - Murder Most Fouled Up (1968)
- ❏ ❏   5 - The Young Can Die Protesting (1969)
- ❏ ❏   6 - Die Quickly, Dear Mother (1969)
- ❏ ❏   7 - Dinky Died (1970)
- ❏ ❏   8 - The Foo Dog (1971)
- ❏ ❏   - Brit.-The Lotus Affair
- ❏ ❏   9 - What To Do Until the Undertaker Comes (1971)

❏❏ 10 - A Die in the Country (1972)
❏❏ 11 - How to Kill a Man (1972)
❏❏ 12 - Brenda's Murder (1973)
❏❏ 13 - Have Mercy Upon Us (1974)
❏❏ 14 - Hark, Hark, the Watchdogs Bark (1975)
❏❏ 15 - A Creature Was Stirring (1977)
❏❏ 16 - Of Graves, Worms and Epitaphs (1988)
❏❏ . . . .
❏❏ . . . .

WENDER, Theodora
Glad Gold & Alden Chase
❏❏ 1 - Knight Must Fall (1985)
❏❏ 2 - Murder Gets a Degree (1986)
❏❏ . . . .
❏❏ . . . .

WESLEY, Valerie Wilson
Tamara Hayle
❏❏ 1 - When Death Comes Stealing (1994)☆
❏❏ 2 - Devil's Gonna Get Him (1995)
❏❏ 3 - Where Evil Sleeps (1996)
❏❏ 4 - No Hiding Place (1997)
❏❏ 5 - Easier To Kill (1998)
❏❏ . . . .
❏❏ . . . .

WESTFALL, Patricia Tichenor
Molly West
❏❏ 1 - Fowl Play (1996)
❏❏ 2 - Mother of the Bride (1998)
❏❏ . . . .
❏❏ . . . .

WESTON, Carolyn
Casey Kellog & Al Krug
❏❏ 1 - Poor, Poor Ophelia (1972)
❏❏ 2 - Susannah Screaming (1975)
❏❏ 3 - Rouse the Demon (1976)
❏❏ . . . .
❏❏ . . . .

WHEAT, Carolyn
Cass Jameson
- ❏ ❏ 1 - Dead Man's Thoughts (1983)☆
- ❏ ❏ 2 - Where Nobody Dies (1986)
- ❏ ❏ 3 - Fresh Kills (1995)
- ❏ ❏ 4 - Mean Streak (1996)
- ❏ ❏ 5 - Troubled Waters (1997)
- ❏ ❏ 6 - Sworn to Defend (1998)
- ❏ ❏ . . . .
- ❏ ❏ . . . .

WHITE, Gloria
Veronica 'Ronnie' Ventana
- ❏ ❏ 1 - Murder on the Run (1991)☆
- ❏ ❏ 2 - Money to Burn (1993)
- ❏ ❏ 3 - Charged With Guilt (1995)☆☆☆
- ❏ ❏ 4 - Sunset and Santiago (1997)☆☆
- ❏ ❏ . . . .
- ❏ ❏ . . . .

WHITE, Teri
Spaceman Kowalski & Blue Maguire
- ❏ ❏ 1 - Bleeding Hearts (1984)
- ❏ ❏ 2 - Tightrope (1986)
- ❏ ❏ . . . .
- ❏ ❏ . . . .

WHITEHEAD, Barbara
Robert Southwell
- ❏ ❏ 1 - Playing God (1988)
- ❏ ❏ 2 - The Girl With Red Suspenders (1990)
- ❏ ❏ 3 - The Dean It Was That Died (1991)
- ❏ ❏ 4 - Sweet Death Come Softly (1992)
- ❏ ❏ 5 - The Killings at Barley Hall (1995)
- ❏ ❏ 6 - Secrets of the Dead (1995)
- ❏ ❏ 7 - Death at the Dutch House (1995)
- ❏ ❏ 8 - Dolls Don't Choose (1998)
- ❏ ❏ . . . .
- ❏ ❏ . . . .

WHITNEY, Polly

Ike Tygart & Abby Abagnarro

❏ ❏   1 - Until Death (1994)☆
❏ ❏   2 - Until the End of Time (1995)
❏ ❏   3 - Until It Hurts (1997)
❏ ❏   4 - Until Pigs Fly (1999)
❏ ❏   . . . .
❏ ❏   . . . .

WILCOX, Valerie

Kellie Montgomery

❏ ❏   1 - Sins of Silence (1998)
❏ ❏   2 - Sins of Betrayal (1999)
❏ ❏   3 - Sins of Deception (2000)
❏ ❏   . . . .
❏ ❏   . . . .

WILHELM, Kate

Barbara Holloway

❏ ❏   1 - Death Qualified (1991)
❏ ❏   2 - The Best Defense (1994)
❏ ❏   3 - Malice Prepense (1996)
❏ ❏   - APA-For the Defense
❏ ❏   4 - Defense for the Devil (1999)
❏ ❏   . . . .
❏ ❏   . . . .

Charlie Meiklejohn & Constance Leidl

❏ ❏   1 - The Hamlet Trap (1987)
❏ ❏   2 - The Dark Door (1988)
❏ ❏   3 - Smart House (1989)
❏ ❏   4 - Sweet, Sweet Poison (1990)
❏ ❏   5 - Seven Kinds of Death (1992)
❏ ❏   6 - A Flush of Shadows [5 novellas] (1995)
❏ ❏   . . . .
❏ ❏   . . . .

WILLIAMS, Amanda Kyle

Madison McGuire

- ❏ ❏   1 - Club Twelve (1990)
- ❏ ❏   2 - The Providence File (1991)
- ❏ ❏   3 - A Singular Spy (1992)
- ❏ ❏   4 - The Spy in Question (1993)
- ❏ ❏   . . . .
- ❏ ❏   . . . .

WILSON, Anne

Sarah Kingsley

- ❏ ❏   1 - Truth or Dare (1995)
- ❏ ❏   2 - Governing Body (1997)
- ❏ ❏   . . . .
- ❏ ❏   . . . .

WILSON, Barbara

Cassandra Reilly

- ❏ ❏   1 - Gaudi Afternoon (1990)★
- ❏ ❏   2 - Trouble in Transylvania (1993)
- ❏ ❏   ss - The Death of a Much-Travelled Woman
        [9 stories] (1998)
- ❏ ❏   . . . .
- ❏ ❏   . . . .

Pam Nilsen

- ❏ ❏   1 - Murder in the Collective (1984)
- ❏ ❏   2 - Sisters of the Road (1986)
- ❏ ❏   3 - The Dog Collar Murders (1989)
- ❏ ❏   . . . .
- ❏ ❏   . . . .

WILSON, Barbara Jaye

Brenda Midnight

- ❏ ❏   1 - Death Brims Over (1997)☆
- ❏ ❏   2 - Accessory to Murder (1998)
- ❏ ❏   3 - Death Flips Its Lid (1998)
- ❏ ❏   . . . .
- ❏ ❏   . . . .

WILSON, Karen Ann

Samantha Holt

❑ ❑ 1 - Eight Dogs Flying (1994)
❑ ❑ 2 - Copy Cat Crimes (1995)
❑ ❑ 3 - Beware Sleeping Dogs (1996)
❑ ❑ 4 - Circle of Wolves (1997)
❑ ❑ . . . .
❑ ❑ . . . .

WILTZ, Chris

Neal Rafferty

❑ ❑ 1 - The Killing Circle (1981)
❑ ❑ 2 - A Diamond Before You Die (1987)
❑ ❑ 3 - The Emerald Lizard (1991)
❑ ❑ . . . .
❑ ❑ . . . .

WINGATE, Anne

Mark Shigata

❑ ❑ 1 - Death by Deception (1988)
❑ ❑ 2 - The Eye of Anna (1989)
❑ ❑ 3 - The Buzzards Must Also Be Fed (1991)
❑ ❑ 4 - Exception to Murder (1992)
❑ ❑ 5 - Yakuza, Go Home! (1993)
❑ ❑ . . . .
❑ ❑ . . . .

WINGS, Mary

Emma Victor

❑ ❑ 1 - She Came Too Late (1986)
❑ ❑ 2 - She Came in a Flash (1988)
❑ ❑ 3 - She Came by the Book (1995)
❑ ❑ 4 - She Came to the Castro (1997)
❑ ❑ . . . .
❑ ❑ . . . .

WINSLOW, Pauline Glen

Merlin Capricorn

❏ ❏ 1 - Death of an Angel (1975)
❏ ❏ 2 - The Brandenburg Hotel (1976)
❏ ❏ 3 - The Witch Hill Murder (1977)
❏ ❏ 4 - Copper Gold (1978)
❏ ❏   - Brit.-Coppergold
❏ ❏ 5 - The Counsellor Heart (1980)
❏ ❏   - APA-Sister Death
❏ ❏ 6 - The Rockefeller Gift (1982)
❏ ❏   . . . .
❏ ❏   . . . .

WOLZIEN, Valerie

Josie Pigeon

❏ ❏ 1 - Shore to Die (1996)
❏ ❏ 2 - Permit for Murder (1997)
❏ ❏ 3 - Deck the Halls With Murder (1998)
❏ ❏   . . . .
❏ ❏   . . . .

Susan Henshaw

❏ ❏ 1 - Murder at the PTA Luncheon (1987)
❏ ❏ 2 - The Fortieth Birthday Body (1989)
❏ ❏ 3 - We Wish You a Merry Murder (1991)
❏ ❏ 4 - All Hallow's Evil (1992)
❏ ❏ 5 - An Old Faithful Murder (1992)
❏ ❏ 6 - A Star-Spangled Murder (1993)
❏ ❏ 7 - A Good Year for a Corpse (1994)
❏ ❏ 8 - Tis the Season To Be Murdered (1994)
❏ ❏ 9 - Remodeled to Death (1995)
❏ ❏ 10 - Elected to Death (1996)
❏ ❏ 11 - Weddings Are Murder (1998)
❏ ❏ 12 - Deck the Halls With Murder (1998)
❏ ❏   . . . .
❏ ❏   . . . .

WOODS, Paula L.

Charlotte Justice

❑ ❑   1 - Inner City Blues (1999)
❑ ❑   2 - Hollywood Swingers (2000)
❑ ❑   . . . .
❑ ❑   . . . .

WOODS, Sherryl

Amanda Roberts

❑ ❑   1 - Reckless (1989)
❑ ❑   2 - Body and Soul (1989)
❑ ❑   3 - Stolen Moments (1990)
❑ ❑   4 - Ties That Bind (1991)
❑ ❑   5 - Bank on It (1993)
❑ ❑   6 - Hide and Seek (1993)
❑ ❑   7 - Wages of Sin (1994)
❑ ❑   8 - Deadly Obsession (1995)
❑ ❑   9 - White Lightning (1995)
❑ ❑   . . . .
❑ ❑   . . . .

Molly DeWitt

❑ ❑   1 - Hot Property (1991)
❑ ❑   2 - Hot Secret (1992)
❑ ❑   3 - Hot Money (1993)
❑ ❑   4 - Hot Schemes (1994)
❑ ❑   . . . .
❑ ❑   . . . .

WOODWARD, Ann

Lady Aoi

❑ ❑   1 - The Exile Way (1996)
❑ ❑   2 - Of Death and Black Rivers (1998)
❑ ❑   . . . .
❑ ❑   . . . .

WOODWORTH, Deborah

Rose Callahan

❏ ❏   1 - Death of a Winter Shaker (1997)
❏ ❏   2 - A Deadly Shaker Spring (1998)
❏ ❏   . . . .
❏ ❏   . . . .

WREN, M. K. [P]

Conan Flagg

❏ ❏   1 - Curiosity Didn't Kill the Cat (1973)
❏ ❏   2 - A Multitude of Sins (1975)
❏ ❏   3 - Oh Bury Me Not (1977)
❏ ❏   4 - Nothing's Certain but Death (1978)
❏ ❏   5 - Seasons of Death (1981)
❏ ❏   6 - Wake Up, Darlin' Corey (1984)
❏ ❏   7 - Dead Matter (1993)
❏ ❏   8 - King of the Mountain (1995)
❏ ❏   . . . .
❏ ❏   . . . .

WRIGHT, L. R.

Eddie Henderson

❏ ❏   1 - Kidnap (1999)
❏ ❏   . . . .
❏ ❏   . . . .

Martin Karl Alberg

❏ ❏   1 - The Suspect (1985)★
❏ ❏   2 - Sleep While I Sing (1986)
❏ ❏   3 - A Chill Rain in January (1990)★
❏ ❏   4 - Fall From Grace (1991)
❏ ❏   5 - Prized Possessions (1993)
❏ ❏   6 - A Touch of Panic (1994)☆
❏ ❏   7 - Mother Love (1995)★
❏ ❏   8 - Strangers Among Us (1996)
❏ ❏   9 - Acts of Murder (1998)
❏ ❏   . . . .
❏ ❏   . . . .

WRIGHT, Nancy Means

Ruth Willmarth

❏ ❏ 1 - Mad Season (1996)
❏ ❏ 2 - Harvest of Bones (1998)
❏ ❏ . . . .
❏ ❏ . . . .

WRIGHT, Sally S.

Ben Reese

❏ ❏ 1 - Publish and Perish (1997)
❏ ❏ 2 - Pride and Predator (1997)
❏ ❏ . . . .
❏ ❏ . . . .

YARBRO, Chelsea Quinn
Charles Spotted Moon
❏ ❏   1 - Ogilvie, Tallant and Moon (1976)
❏ ❏   - APA-Bad Medicine (1990)
❏ ❏   2 - Music When Sweet Voices Die (1979)
❏ ❏   - APA-False Notes (1990)
❏ ❏   3 - Poison Fruit (1991)
❏ ❏   4 - Cat's Claw (1992)
❏ ❏   . . . .
❏ ❏   . . . .

YEAGER, Dorian
Elizabeth Will
❏ ❏   1 - Murder Will Out (1994)
❏ ❏   2 - Summer Will End (1995)
❏ ❏   . . . .
❏ ❏   . . . .

Victoria Bowering
❏ ❏   1 - Cancellation by Death (1992)
❏ ❏   2 - Eviction by Death (1993)
❏ ❏   3 - Ovation by Death (1996)
❏ ❏   4 - Libation by Death (1998)
❏ ❏   . . . .
❏ ❏   . . . .

YORK, Kieran
Royce Madison
❏ ❏   1 - Timber City Masks (1993)
❏ ❏   2 - Crystal Mountain Veils (1995)
❏ ❏   . . . .
❏ ❏   . . . .

YORKE, Margaret [P]
Patrick Grant
❏ ❏ 1 - Dead in the Morning (1970)
❏ ❏ 2 - Silent Witness (1972)
❏ ❏ 3 - Grave Matters (1973)
❏ ❏ 4 - Mortal Remains (1974)
❏ ❏ 5 - Cast for Death (1976)
❏ ❏ . . . .
❏ ❏ . . . .

YOUMANS, Claire
Janet Schilling
❏ ❏ 1 - Rough Justice (1996)
❏ ❏ 2 - Rough Trip (1999)
❏ ❏ . . . .
❏ ❏ . . . .

Sandy Whitacre
❏ ❏ 1 - The First Death (1999)
❏ ❏ . . . .
❏ ❏ . . . .

ZACHARY, Fay

Liz Broward & Zack James

- ❏ ❏ 1 - Blood Work (1994)
- ❏ ❏ 2 - A Poison in the Blood (1994)
- ❏ ❏ . . . .
- ❏ ❏ . . . .

ZAREMBA, Eve

Helen Karemos

- ❏ ❏ 1 - A Reason to Kill (1978)
- ❏ ❏ 2 - Work for a Million (1987)
- ❏ ❏ 3 - Beyond Hope (1988)
- ❏ ❏ 4 - Uneasy Lies (1990)
- ❏ ❏ 5 - The Butterfly Effect (1994)
- ❏ ❏ . . . .
- ❏ ❏ . . . .

ZUKOWSKI, Sharon

Blaine Stewart

- ❏ ❏ 1 - The Hour of the Knife (1991)
- ❏ ❏ 2 - Dancing in the Dark (1992)
- ❏ ❏ 3 - Leap of Faith (1994)
- ❏ ❏ 4 - Prelude to Death (1996)
- ❏ ❏ 5 - Jungleland (1997)
- ❏ ❏ . . . .
- ❏ ❏ . . . .

NOTES

Don't miss the new BIG book. Better than ever in an all new hardcover 3rd edition.

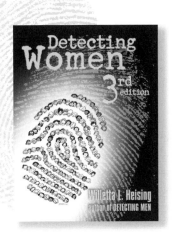

The most comprehensive guide available for women's detective fiction with more than 500 new series mysteries published in 1998-1999. Fascinating 150-word biographies for more than 650 living women authors, including American, British, Canadian and Australian novelists. Along with complete lists of mysteries in correct series order, you'll find easy-to-use indexes for characters, settings, mystery types, book titles and dates of publication. Complete information is also provided for mystery awards and author pseudonyms.

Willetta L. Heising's *"immensely popular...ever-helpful"* *(Washington Post BookWorld)* reader's guides are fast becoming standards in the mystery field. Her earlier titles have won two Agatha Awards, a pair of Macavity Awards, an Anthony Award and an Edgar nomination for nonfiction.

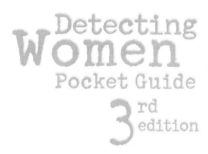

Detecting Women
Pocket Guide
3rd edition

The most comprehensive guide available for women's detective fiction with more than 500 new series mysteries published in 1998-1999. Fascinating 150-word biographies for more than 650 living women authors, including American, British, Canadian and Australian novelists. Along with complete lists of mysteries in correct series order, you'll find easy-to-use indexes for characters, settings, mystery types, book titles and dates of publication. Complete information is also provided for mystery awards and author pseudonyms.

"A need-to-know nugget on every page."
Amazon.com Recommended Book

"Probably the most useful reference on my bookshelf."
Mystery Collectors' BookList

Detecting Women, 3rd Edition   ISBN 0-9644593-5-3
448 pages, 8½ by 11 inches, *hardcover edition*, $44.95

softcover edition, $34.95   ISBN 0-9644593-6-1
available November 1998, copyright 1999

PURPLE
MOON
PRESS

Purple Moon Press
3319 Greenfield Rd., Suite 317
Dearborn, Michigan 48120-1212

Visit our website at <www.purplemoonpress.com